LIFE LESSONS

FOR YOUNG ADOLESCENTS

An Advisory Guide for Teachers

Fred Schrumpf • Sharon Freiburg • David Skadden

Research Press   2612 North Mattis Avenue   Champaign, Illinois 61822
(800) 519-2707   www.researchpress.com

Cover design by Linda Brown
Composition by BookMasters, Inc.
Printed by Malloy Lithographing

ISBN 0–87822–343–6
Library of Congress Catalog No. 93–83884

To our ''life lesson'' advisors, our parents:

Ann and Ben Schrumpf

Shirley and Jack Freiburg

Barbara and Don Skadden

Contents

Unit Three: Celebrate Yourself

Unit Four: Communication and Conflict Resolution

Unit Five: Relating to Others

Unit Six: Your Community

Acknowledgments

This manual began in 1987 at Urbana Middle School in Urbana, Illinois, with a committee of teachers and support service staff members who developed a philosophy and rationale for advisory groups, as well as many of the activities presented in this book. Each year the program was evaluated, revised, and augmented. We appreciate the commitment and dedication of the following individuals in these efforts: Val Summerville, Katie Bridges, Marilyn Mastny, Chu Usadel, Brian Kahn, and Connie Minnes. We also acknowledge the administrative support and vision of Dr. Henry Meares, who strongly believed in the importance of an advisory program.

More ideas, suggestions, and support were given by other outstanding professionals in the fields of education and counseling: Gaye Dunn, Topper Steinman, and Michele Agusti. Additional colleagues and friends who have given guidance include Karen DeVoss, Kathy Rose, Doris Malacarne, Deb Schrock, Phyllis Gingold, and Carol McGehe.

Finally, we are grateful for the support and understanding of our inner circle of family: Chris Dunn, Golie Jansen, Kim Smith, Spencer, Vincent, Will, Anneke, and Michael. Without them, this book could not have been written.

Introduction

There is no doubt that children are coming to school more in need than ever of strong academic instruction. However, the youth we teach are also more in need than ever of support, nurturing, and the life skills necessary for success. Today, classroom teachers are expected to teach academic content, as well as provide social-emotional support and life skills training so students can cope with the risks of growing up.

Across the country, teachers at the middle grades are being asked to be advisors as well as instructors to their students. The teacher is expected to teach the whole child, showing awareness of the cognitive as well as the affective self. The National Middle School Association (1982) and the National Association of Secondary School Principals (1985) assert the need for strong guidance and advisory programs. These advisement programs would provide compassionate support and careful attention to students' social and personal development. *Turning Points: Preparing American Youth for the 21st Century* states that middle schools need to have "small group advisories that ensure that every student is known well by at least one adult" (Carnegie Council on Adolescent Development, 1989, p. 40).

Teachers will agree that their students need support and help to master various life skills, but how exactly this should take place remains a question. Teacher as adviser is a new role—and one for which many teachers feel unprepared.

THE ADVISORY PROGRAM: CENTRAL ASSUMPTIONS

Advisory programs are designed with a primary prevention and wellness approach. The central assumptions of such programs are as follows:

1. Students bring many risk factors to school—poverty, divorce, substance abuse in the family, disability, racism, violence, and so forth. These risk factors affect their attitude toward learning.

2. It is possible for students to learn certain prosocial skills to increase their resiliency to these risk factors. Such skills concern communication, coping with stress, decision making/problem solving, and conflict resolution. Responsibility and self-direction can be taught and learned.

3. Students need to feel secure at school. Positive interaction with adults and peers gives students a sense of belonging, vital to a positive school climate.

4. Educating the whole child leads to the development of good citizens. These are individuals who have the skills to handle their own problems, conflicts, and challenges.

5. Developing life skills is accomplished by doing and experiencing. The process is interactive and cooperative—shared by student and teacher.

6. Academic success will accompany healthy social-emotional growth.

ORGANIZATION OF THE ADVISORY PROGRAM

Implementing an advisory program involves making decisions about staff training, curriculum materials, format and scheduling, parent information, and ongoing support and supervision. Some schools have very well-developed advisory programs, whereas other schools are in the planning stage.

The cornerstone of the advisory program is the advisory group. If the entire staff—including resource teachers, support services, and administration—is involved, students can be divided into groups smaller than the typical class. It is easier to develop close relationships and trust within a smaller group. In addition, smaller groups help foster open communication, understanding, and acceptance among members.

The advisory program can be delivered in various ways. Some advisory programs include lessons within classroom curricula; most subject areas can adopt an applied and personalized approach to include life skills. The most common delivery model involves incorporating advisory lessons into the homeroom period. Homeroom advisory classes meet every day for 20 minutes or so. With this model, some days are spent on discussions and activities. Others are for homework checks, getting organized, or silent reading. Some schools rotate an advisory period throughout the class schedule. Such periods are generally longer, up to 40 minutes, and meet one to three times a week.

Whatever the schedule, the general themes of the advisory group remain the same. Commonly, these include the following:

1. Getting acquainted, school adjustment, group/team identity

2. Academic success and study skills

3. Self-esteem and coping

4. Communicating and problem solving

5. Relationships

6. Community involvement and citizenship

7. Career exploration

A successful advisory group will also employ a student-teacher dialogue format, with many student-generated questions. Encourage students to write anonymous questions or concerns and drop them in a designated box in your room. Throughout the year, these questions can be discussed and used to encourage group problem-solving.

OVERVIEW OF UNIT THEMES

This book has been written to help teachers called upon to be advisers learn to fill this role. It includes short, simple activities that deal in a practical way with everyday concerns of young adolescents. Most are designed to be completed in 20 to 30 minutes and to use readily available materials. Primarily intended for use in the advisory group setting, the activities can also be used in classes covering topics such as self-awareness, communication, decision making, or peer relationships—for example, health, home economics, language arts, or social science.

The activities are organized into six units. Because the six units are not sequential, they may be used independently and in any order. Teachers should feel free to choose activities from each of the units or to adapt activities as necessary.

Unit One: Building a Team

The main activities in this unit are preceded by a number of "boundary breakers" and group energizers lasting from 5 to 10 minutes each. These short activities are designed to offer a low-risk way for group members to get acquainted. They can be used throughout the year to help the group stay energized and relaxed. The other activities provided in this unit are designed to establish the group's purpose and ground rules and to help participants get to know one another better.

Unit Two: School Success

School success begins when students know their school, school rules, and expectations. Unit Two offers activities to help students in this area. Activities include situational role-plays to promote good choices when school challenges arise. In addition, they suggest ways to help students set academic goals, stay organized, and complete homework assignments.

Unit Three: Celebrate Yourself

The activities in this unit are focused on self. Specifically, they reflect on issues of self-esteem (fitting in, self-talk, fears, strengths), individual behaviors (habits, boredom, motivation), and emotions (happiness, guilt, hate, embarrassment).

Unit Four: Communication and Conflict Resolution

This unit focuses on the life skills of communication, decision-making, and conflict resolution. Because of increased violence and conflict in schools, conflict resolution skills are increasingly important. Much of conflict resolution is based on clear communication and problem-solving skills. These skills can be learned—the activities in this unit are designed to help teach them.

Unit Five: Relating to Others

Peer relationships are very important to young adolescents, and discussions within the peer group can help clarify the importance of relationships and how to make and keep friends. The activities in this unit address this issue and also explore cultural and individual differences to increase understanding among the various groups within the school.

Unit Six: Your Community

Students need to be made aware of their community and how to contribute to it. This unit provides activities to promote community awareness of social agencies, businesses, and local government. Activities presented also concern the type of jobs and careers available and suggest ways to involve students in the community through volunteer projects.

Units Two, Three, Four, and Five each include a section entitled "Words for Discussion." The purpose of these discussion words is for students first to *personalize* the word. Then students *define* the word as they see it. Finally, they think about how the word applies to them (the *challenge*). These discussions take little or no preparation and usually promote lively interchange.

WORKING WITH THE ADVISORY GROUP

In order to lead a successful group with young adolescents, it is important to understand the young adolescent and to master some basic group facilitation skills. This section briefly discusses the adolescent and the role of adult as facilitator and key to relationship building for youths. In addition, it describes some common group problems and their solutions.

Understanding the Young Adolescent

"I'm bored," "I can't find my homework," "It's not fair," "Who's she going with?" "I can't help it," and "It's not my fault." These typical statements reflect the young adolescent's need to cope with self-doubt, status among peers, and physical changes while struggling with new independence, turbulent emotions, and developing sex roles. At no other time in life does an individual encounter so many diverse problems simultaneously.

This challenging developmental age is best characterized by rapid change. The physical, social, and emotional selves are very different from those in previous years. Great variability and diversity can be seen in the development of each youth. Reading levels may range from the third- to twelfth-grade levels. Thinking will range from very concrete to higher level abstract thought. Some girls still await the onset of puberty, whereas others have already given birth.

These are years of new independence and learning by trial and error. Peer relationships become critical in the young adolescent's new search for identity. Peers are the source of a great deal of the information and misinformation a young adolescent will use in the development of self. Because of both environmental and personal changes, this is a high-risk developmental stage.

In this context, the new social skills of communication, decision making, and critical thinking become vital. Relationships with adults are still very important, even though the young person is trying to separate from his or her most significant adults—parents. In a world with widespread access to television, movies, videos, music, and magazines, the young adolescent is being exposed to and is making decisions in areas once considered "adults only." Few would argue that these are challenging times for the youth as well as for those who work with this age group.

Basic Group Facilitation Skills

The facilitator is the person most directly responsible for leading the group and most intimately concerned with the social, emotional, intellectual, and physical well-being of group members. Specifically, the facilitator attempts to accomplish the following goals:

1. Build a relationship with each student characterized by caring, trust, and honesty

2. Listen to the ideas and concerns of students and help them find answers to questions and resolve problems

3. Provide an environment for the group that will build cooperation and understanding

4. Prepare activities and discussions that will implement the purpose of the advisory program

5. Communicate with parents the purpose of the group and the skills being learned

6. Encourage students to be responsible for a quality academic performance

7. Refer students to additional academic or social services when needed

8. Encourage different points of view

9. Encourage students' self-evaluation of behavioral and academic performance

10. Be a positive role model for youths

Characteristics of the Successful Group Facilitator

The Group Facilitator's Self-Evaluation Checklist, on the next page, lists the main characteristics needed to work effectively with groups. The more frequently an adult demonstrates these characteristics, the more successful he or she will be as a group facilitator.

Establishing Positive Relationships

In general, the focus of any group should be on listening and being "real." Relationships are built on honesty, openness, and caring. As a teacher and group leader, it is hard always to be at your best.

GROUP FACILITATOR'S SELF-EVALUATION CHECKLIST

1. Enjoys being with young people.

    Usually ☐ Sometimes ☐ Rarely ☐

2. Shows interest and enthusiasm.

    Usually ☐ Sometimes ☐ Rarely ☐

3. Can spark students' interest in the challenges of life.

    Usually ☐ Sometimes ☐ Rarely ☐

4. Will try new things and take risks.

    Usually ☐ Sometimes ☐ Rarely ☐

5. Is honest, trustworthy, and willing to share feelings.

    Usually ☐ Sometimes ☐ Rarely ☐

6. Is prepared and positive.

    Usually ☐ Sometimes ☐ Rarely ☐

7. Looks forward to each day.

    Usually ☐ Sometimes ☐ Rarely ☐

8. Believes all students can learn responsibility and prosocial skills.

    Usually ☐ Sometimes ☐ Rarely ☐

9. Helps students apply problem-solving and decision-making skills to real-life situations.

    Usually ☐ Sometimes ☐ Rarely ☐

10. Helps students evaluate and reach their academic potential.

    Usually ☐ Sometimes ☐ Rarely ☐

11. Attempts to promote positive self-esteem in all students.

    Usually ☐ Sometimes ☐ Rarely ☐

12. Models a positive attitude about life and others.

    Usually ☐ Sometimes ☐ Rarely ☐

Some students are easier to work with than others. However, being positive and caring will go a long way with most young people. Having a healthy relationship with a positive adult role model is the best way for a young person to learn responsibility and prosocial skills.

Most of the activities presented in this book are designed to help promote group bonding and understanding and to encourage the development of sharing and thinking skills. Students will master the necessary information much more easily if there is a positive climate established in the group. The facilitator is critical in building trust and positive relationships among participants and in setting the tone for the learning process. The following suggestions may help in this effort:

1. Take time at the beginning of the year to explain the purpose of the group. Tell students that you are all here to:

   Talk

   Listen

   Respect one another

   Share ideas and feelings

   Learn to solve problems and resolve conflicts

   Have fun

   Care about one another, both academically and socially

2. Emphasize to students that any questions or concerns they might have are real and that the group is the time and place to share them.

3. Take the time to do as many boundary breakers, energizers, and getting-to-know-one-another activities as it takes to make the group feel comfortable (see Unit One). These activities can be done throughout the year.

4. During all discussions, be sure to participate yourself. If you are willing to share, your students will be encouraged to share. Your positive model is important to a successful group. Share appropriate personal experiences, thoughts, and feelings with your students.

5. Take time to get to know each student individually. Write personal notes to acknowledge individual accomplishments, birthdays, or problems you might be aware of—or just to say, "Hello, and make it a good day."

6. Have fun!

Working Cooperatively in Small Groups

As is the case in the general classroom, many times a larger group will need to divide into smaller working units. Usually these smaller units range from three to five students each. Smaller working groups can be formed randomly, or you can preassign students to the groups.

In smaller cooperative groups, students can learn from one another and practice leadership and responsibility. Learning to work together toward a common goal is team-building and personally rewarding.

More students will get involved in the learning and discussions. In addition, friendships will develop that might not otherwise have occurred, thus promoting a more positive group and school climate.

Our world is made of many different kinds of people, and students need to learn how to deal with a variety of personalities. Therefore, it is important that smaller working groups reflect the diversity of the larger group as much as possible. In addition to maintaining diversity, another goal in creating smaller groups is for each student to work with every other student by the end of a semester. Ensuring such interaction will help build the support system necessary for success in the group.

The following ideas for creating smaller working groups may be helpful:

1. Deal a deck of playing cards to the larger group. Group all the fives together, all the clubs together, and so forth.

2. Place students with zippers or a certain number of buttons together. Look clothes over carefully and quickly determine if you can use shirt color to form groups of equal size.

3. Have students identify their favorite pizza place. Put all the Pizza Huts together, all the Dominos together, all the Godfathers together, and so on. (You can also group students by favorite kind of pizza.)

4. Group students by the color of the family car.

5. Assign students by the kind or number of writing utensils they have brought to your class.

6. Have students line up by order of birthday. Then count them off to form groups.

7. Give students a number as they enter the room. Use these numbers to form groups.

8. Use the number of siblings to determine groups.

9. Assess shoes: Put all the leathers together, all the high-tops together, and so forth. You can also establish groups by the kinds of fabrics students are wearing—all the cottons together, all the wools together, all the denims together, and so on.

10. List a variety of vacation spots. Have students select which spot they would most like to visit. Assign groups by these selections.

11. Have half of the class put their names in a hat. Have the other half draw out a name.

12. Group students by the form of transportation they use in getting to school (bus riders, walkers, bike riders, and so on).

13. Assign students to groups by the first letters of their names. Mark, Mike, Marsha, and Micah are all together. Julie, Jack, Jane, and Jermaine are all together. You can use the second letter or the last letter if that works best for your group.

14. Go by birthdays: All the January babies are together, all the February babies are together, and so forth.

15. Send students home to find out the day of the week they were born. Place all in groups accordingly.

16. Form groups by favorite school subjects. All math lovers can work together today, all social studies lovers can work together tomorrow, and so on.

17. Create groups by the direction they need to go to get home.

Common Group Problems and Solutions

The following discussion details some common group problems and their solutions. It is important, however, to realize that group facilitation is a challenge. Any problem in group dynamics can be overcome, but there are no "quick fix" solutions. Many of the topics handled in groups will spark unresolved issues for us as adults. Therefore, teachers should get together and talk about their groups with one another and with resource staff.

Problem: A student talks too much.

Solution: Equalizing "air time" is often a problem in groups. It is important to point out that everybody has good ideas and that it is necessary to give everyone a chance to share. Going around the circle helps give everyone a chance. In open discussions, you can also make a rule that no one can make a second comment until everyone has made a first comment.

Problem: One student does not talk.

Solution: It is probably best to talk to this student individually to see if he or she is uncomfortable in the group or with the topic of discussion. Establish routines where everyone gets a chance to make a comment before discussion is open to the whole group. When brainstorming is used, call upon the quiet student. This is a low-risk way of making a comment.

Problem: Students are disrespectful or disruptive while in group.

Solution: It is always a good idea to go back to group rules and expectations about respecting others. Often this disruptive energy can be used in a leadership or helper role if the facilitator structures it in a positive way. It also can be very helpful to talk to the student individually and ask for cooperation. Often the disruptive student needs some of your individual time for relationship building.

Problem: There is no energy or zest in the group.

Solution: Many boundary breaker and energizer activities can get students up, moving, and involved again. If a discussion is going nowhere, change the plan and try an energizer.

Problem: A student shares inappropriate information.

Solution: Students may bring up a number of personal issues. If you don't feel comfortable with the topic, probably other students don't feel comfortable with it either. It is best just to say, "This is not appropriate for group, and I will talk to you about it later."

Problem: A student has a problem that needs to be referred.

Solution: Most schools have counselors, social workers, and psychologists who are trained to deal with more difficult or recurring problems that need specialized interventions. You can seek consultation from these support service professionals. It is important to advise the student that you feel a referral is necessary and help the student connect with the appropriate resource person.

Decision Making and Brainstorming

A number of the activities in Unit Four use a decision-making model and the technique of brainstorming. *Decision making* is the process of solving problems, handling challenges, and making choices. If we make good decisions, we will move toward our goals. If we do not make decisions or make them poorly, we will fall short of the expectations we hope to achieve.

Many adolescents are impulsive and lack the ability to reason logically. They have difficulty making sound decisions. Often the choices they make lead to bigger problems, which lead to even more difficult decisions. It is therefore important that, over the course of the school year, we teach and reteach a decision-making model that works for students. Briefly, the steps in this decision-making model are as follows.

Step 1: Define the Problem

What is the problem as you see it?

Is there also an underlying issue?

What are the causes of the problem?

What do you want to see happen?

Step 2: Think of Possible Options

What are all the options you have?

What have you tried in the past?

Be creative—there are more options than you think.

Step 3: Review Your Options and Choose One

Examine the risks, benefits, and consequences of each idea.

Look at short-term and long-term effects.

Choose the one or two options you are willing to try.

Step 4: Act on Your Choice

What is your plan?

What do you need to do in order for this decision to work?

What are the benefits of your plan?

Do you need help from anyone to make the plan work?

Step 5: Evaluate Your Actions

Did your plan work?

What did you learn from your decision?

Do you need to change your plan or try something else?

One way teachers can facilitate students' acquisition of decision-making skills is by waiting before giving answers or opinions. Instead, teachers need to ask the questions used in the decision-making process. This way, students will learn to use these steps in various everyday situations.

Step 2 of the decision-making process just described relies on *brainstorming* all possible options. Whenever brainstorming is part of a group activity, you should review some basic rules. It is a good idea to have the following rules written on either the chalkboard or a poster:

1. Say any ideas that come to mind.

2. Don't judge or discuss the ideas.

3. Build on all the ideas given.

4. Be spontaneous and creative.

5. Come up with as many ideas as possible.

After a list of ideas is generated, a general discussion can take place. Ideas can be combined or disregarded when looking for a solution.

UNIT ONE

Building a Team

In my life, if you have a purpose in which you can believe,
there's no end to the amount of things you can accomplish.

Marian Anderson

Overview

This unit provides activities designed to help group members get to know one another, understand the purpose of the group, and bond as a unit.

The first part describes boundary breakers and energizers. These brief exercises are designed to offer a low-risk way for group members to interact and feel comfortable with one another. They involve movement and a high level of participation by all group members, last from 5 to 10 minutes, and involve few if any materials. All of these exercises will help a group stay energized and relaxed. After an exercise is completed, time can be spent discussing how people felt and what was learned during the experience. An exercise can also be used just for the fun of it. Especially good for "breaking the ice" in the beginning, these exercises can help revitalize the group at any time.

It is important to establish the purpose of the group and ground rules or expectations as soon as possible. Therefore, the first two full-length activities in this unit focus on explaining the group's purpose and setting group guidelines.

The remaining activities are designed to help group members get to know one another better. They begin with simply learning names and progress to sharing personal information and ideas.

Boundary Breakers and Energizers

I LIKE PEOPLE WHO . . .

Purpose To help members of your group become better acquainted

Materials Chairs in a circle, with one fewer chair than the number of group members

Procedure One student stands in the middle of the circle of chairs. All the other students are seated. The sender gives his or her name, then says, "I like people who . . . " He or she fills in the blank with a description such as "have blue jeans" or "have brown hair." Students who fit that description must stand up and run for an empty seat. The person left standing in the middle repeats the activity: "My name is . . . and I like people who . . . "

EXTENSION CORD CONFUSION

Purpose To encourage teamwork and problem-solving skills

Materials One 50- to 100-foot extension cord for each group of 20 participants

Procedure The extension cord(s) is knotted several times. Each person within the group is asked to place one hand on a section of the cord. The group must then untangle the cord without removing their hands.

THE CROWDED TELEPHONE BOOTH

Purpose To solve a group problem

Materials Masking tape

Procedure Place masking tape on the floor in the shape of a square to represent a telephone booth. Depending on the size of the group, the square can be big or small—be sure to make it a bit too small for participants to fit in comfortably. The objective of the exercise is to get the whole group within the boundaries of the square. This can be done by forming any configuration that the group wants to try.

Note. Extension Cord Confusion, The Crowded Telephone Booth, One-Minute Interview, Spider Web, Animal Farm, Line-Up, Skin the Snake, and Who Am I? have been adapted by permission from activities appearing in *Boundary Breakers: A Team Building Guide for Student Activity Advisers,* by J. Schrader, 1990, Reston, VA: National Association of Secondary School Principals. This resource also contains many other good activities.

ONE-MINUTE INTERVIEW

Purpose   To develop listening and communication skills

Materials   None

Procedure   Everyone in the group is instructed to find a partner that he or she does not know very well. One is the speaker and the other is the listener. The listener gets a minute to find out all he or she can about the speaker. After the minute, the listener shares with the group all the information discovered. Listener and speaker then switch roles.

SPIDER WEB

Purpose   To have fun and learn something new about others

Materials   Ball of yarn

Procedure   Ask the group to sit in a circle. One person begins the activity by stating his or her name and something that he or she likes to do. (For example, "My name is Fred, and I like to play tennis.") While holding the end of a ball of yarn, the person tosses the ball to someone else in the circle. That person states his or her name and something he or she likes to do. This continues until everyone has received the ball of yarn and a spider web has been created. Point out how everyone is connected in the group. Each student can break the yarn where he or she is holding it and take a piece to remember the group's connectedness. Some might even make a bracelet from the yarn.

ANIMAL FARM

Purpose   To get into cooperative working groups of four in a fun way

Materials   An index card for each group member

Procedure   On groups of four index cards, write a separate animal sound. Randomly hand out one card to each person. Participants walk around the room making the animal noise on the card. It will sound like a barnyard: "Oink-oink," "moo-moo," and "quack-quack" all at the same time. When the group of four have found one another, ask them to sit down.

LINE-UP

Purpose   To get acquainted and learn to follow directions

Materials   None

Procedure   Ask the group to line up in a semicircle as quickly as possible based on the directions given. A good direction to start with is "Line up in alphabetical order." Other possible commands would ask students to line up by birthday, height, miles traveled this summer, and so forth. (Be creative!)

SKIN THE SNAKE

Purpose   To develop teamwork

Materials   None

Procedure   Ask the group to form a single line facing forward. Each participant takes his or her right hand, putting it back between his or her legs and taking the left hand of the person behind. The last person in line lies down while still holding the hand of the person in front of him or her. Each person in line then steps backward while straddling the person lying down, still holding hands, until this process has all group members lying down. Group members reverse the process, and the last to lie down is the first to get up. The first person walks forward until all group members, with hands joined, have gotten up from the floor.

CLASSROOM CAROLING

Purpose   To break up cliques or break into groups

Materials   One index card for each participant

Procedure   Write the title of a well-known Christmas song, such as "Jingle Bells," on groups of four index cards. Pass cards out to all participants. Ask them to walk around the room singing their song and looking for another person singing the same song. Once a group is fully formed, have members sing a chorus of their carol.

FOLLOW THE BOUNCING BALL

Purpose To help participants take turns and learn to be patient when they have something to say

Materials A sponge ball, beach ball, or playground ball

Procedure Have everyone sit in a circle and discuss a controversial subject. Each person is allowed to speak at any time he or she is holding the ball. When the speaker is finished, he or she passes the ball to someone else. This way only one person can talk at a time.

WHO AM I?

Purpose Mixer

Materials Index cards with character names and pins or tape

Procedure Pin or tape the name of a famous person or fictional character on the back of each participant without letting that person see the name. These names could include Madonna, Babe Ruth, Michael Jackson, Minnie Mouse, George Washington, and so forth. Each person is to answer the question "Who am I?" by asking questions of others in the group. Rules for the questions:

1. Each participant may ask only three questions of the others, who must answer truthfully.

2. Only yes/no questions are allowed. For example: "Am I a real person?" "Am I dead?" "Am I female?" "Am I a 'good' character?"

   When someone finds out an identity, he or she may put the name on the front. These people may continue to answer questions for others.

HUMAN MACHINES

Purpose To spark creativity and have fun

Materials None

Procedure Divide the class into groups of four to six. Each group is to think of a machine and create it, complete with movement and sound effects. They can use only their bodies and the sounds they can make. Give each group 5 minutes for practice. Have each group demonstrate their machine and encourage the others to guess what machine it is. You can also give each group a slip of paper suggesting the machine they are to represent. For example: garbage disposal, vacuum cleaner, washing machine, pencil sharpener, motorcycle, and school bus.

SEND A FAX

Purpose   To teach listening skills and have fun

Materials   None

Procedure   Have the group get into a circle. Whisper a message into the ear of the person to your left. You should whisper the message only once. The student then passes what he or she heard along to the person to the left, and so on, until the phrase comes around to the person on your right. Repeat the message that made it around the circle out loud. See how the message has changed. Try again.

ONE, TWO, THREE, FOUR

Purpose   To help build cooperation within a group

Materials   None

Procedure   Ask the group to form smaller groups of three. Participants face one another holding a clenched fist. Then they shake their fists up and down together four times and chant together, "One, two, three, four!" On the count of four, each one puts out any number of fingers from zero to 5. The object of this activity is for the three to have a total of 11 fingers out. They repeat until they succeed. Once they total 11, have them use two fists and try getting to 23, putting out any number of fingers from zero to 10. You can write a series of numbers on the board for each group to total.

I CAN'T GO TO SCHOOL TODAY BECAUSE . . .

Purpose   To learn brainstorming and be creative

Materials   Chalkboard

Procedure   Have the students form pairs. Write the following sentence on the board: "Mom, I can't go to school today because: I've got acne, backache, and chronic coughing." Point out that the description of the ailments isn't random. The excuses for not going to school are in alphabetical order: A for acne, B for backache, and C for chronic coughing. Go around the room and ask each pair to think of one more word to add to the end of the sentence. Write the new word or phrase on the board and read back the whole sentence to the class. Then it is the next pair's turn to add a word. Students will enjoy their chance to be creative and have fun lining up all their excuses!

PRETZEL

Purpose To teach group communication and problem solving

Materials None

Procedure This energizer involves two teams of 5 to 15 people each. One person from each team leaves the room, and each team forms a circle, holding hands. Each team now takes a minute or so to form a "pretzel." This is done by continuing to hold hands and entwining (people passing under arms, stepping over, etc.) until the team is a mass of bodies, still linked. The other people are now invited back in. Their job is to untangle the two teams, who must obey all instructions. People cannot break handholds when they are untangling. Don't take longer than the group's energy allows—3 or 4 minutes—because people may become tired holding their positions in the pretzel.

TAKE A DEEP BREATH

Purpose To help students learn names

Materials None

Procedure Have the group form a circle. One student volunteer takes a deep breath and begins walking around the circle, pointing at each person and saying the person's name. The goal is to say everyone's name before taking another breath. The person's success will depend not only upon lung capacity but also on the size of the circle. Continue until everyone has had a turn or the activity loses its energy.

TAKE ME TO YOUR LEADER

Purpose To increase observation skills

Materials None

Procedure Ask one student to leave the room for a minute. After the student is gone, have the class stand in a circle and choose one person who will be the leader. The leader begins to perform a series of physical signs (clapping, snapping, foot tapping, hand movements, winks, etc.) that the others imitate and that change every 10 seconds. Ask the student to return and try to guess who the leader is by observing the group. Let him or her have three guesses. Repeat the process by asking for another student to leave the room and choosing another leader.

THE DREAM JOB

Purpose   To help students think about the future and practice visualization

Materials   None

Procedure   Have the students sit in a circle. Tell them to relax and use their imaginations. Say, "Imagine yourself doing the job you'd like to be doing 10 years from now. Where would you work? What would you be responsible for?" Go around the circle and share briefly what this job would be. You can ask students to use their imaginations for questions relating to other topics (for example, traveling to an exciting place, going to a calm place, seeing something they always wanted to see).

WHAT'S IN THE BOX?

Purpose   To promote group cooperation and problem solving

Materials   A shoe box with any 25 common household items in it (for example, a battery, thumbtack, quarter, golf ball, ping-pong ball, rubber band, fingernail file)

Procedure   Have the large group get into smaller groups of four. Tell the smaller groups that you have 25 items in the shoe box and you are going to give each group 30 seconds to look in the box. After the time is up, groups are to try to remember all the items they saw in the box. Let groups plan a few minutes to see how they will approach this problem. Have each group come to the box one at a time and silently view the contents for 30 seconds. Then have them return to their seats and write down the item names. After 5 minutes, hold up each item and see if the groups remembered it. Ask each group how well they did and how they approached the problem.

Activities

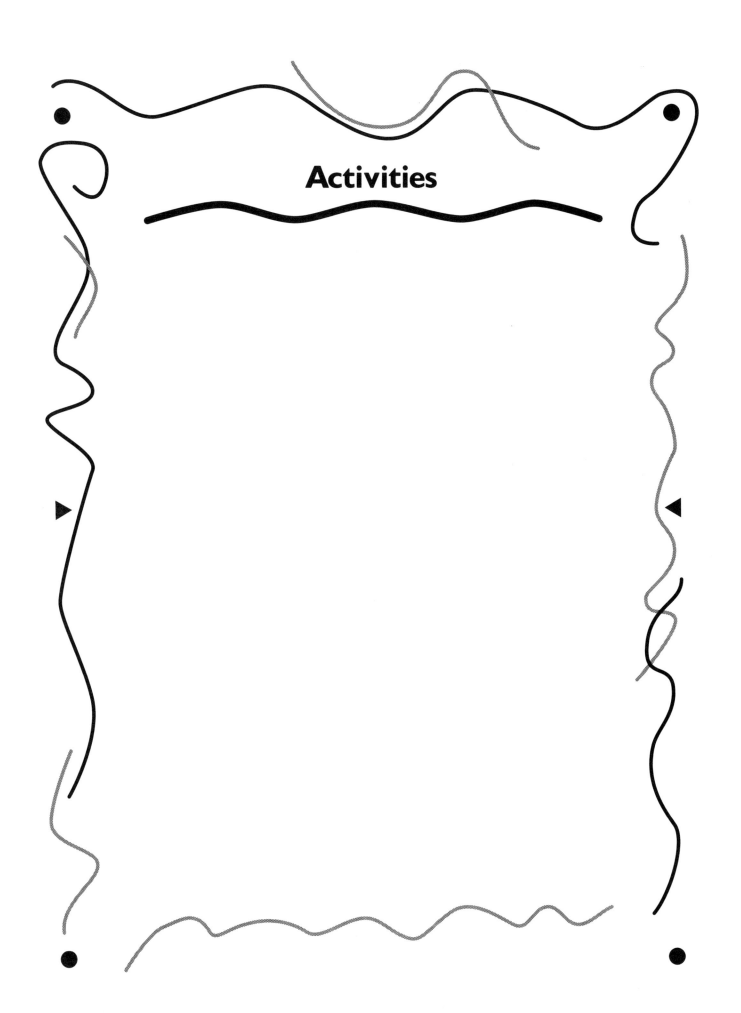

The Purpose of an Advisory Group

Purpose To acquaint students with the purpose of the advisory group

Materials Chalkboard
Student Information and Interest Inventory (Handout 1)

Procedure 1. Start out with one of the boundary breaker/energizer activities.

2. Write the following words on the chalkboard: *talk, listen, trust, support, respect, care, fun,* and *solve problems.* Explain in your own words the reasons for an advisory group and how these words on the board summarize the focus.

3. Explain that the group will be doing a lot of activities and having discussions on many topics. Stress that you also hope to improve communication skills and help students learn how to solve problems and work out conflicts.

4. State that there will be time to talk about school and how to be successful at school. School is the students' job, and they will feel better about themselves if they are successful at school. This success involves both their academic and social performance.

5. Have students fill out the Student Information and Interest Inventory (Handout 1). Collect and keep these for future reference.

Handout 1

STUDENT INFORMATION AND INTEREST INVENTORY

Name _____

Age _____ Birthday _____

Phone number _____ Locker number _____

Address _____

List the people you live with and your relationship to them:

_____

_____

_____

Which schools have you attended before? _____

_____

Favorite food _____

Hobbies _____

Favorite TV show _____

Favorite subject in school _____

Favorite movie _____

What you do for fun _____

Favorite place you have visited _____

School activities _____

Class Schedule

	Class	Teacher	Room number
1.			
2.			
3.			
4.			
5.			
6.			
7.			
8.			

Rules for Advisory Groups

Purpose   To establish some ground rules and expectations for the group

Materials   Chalkboard
Poster board and markers

Procedure   1. Review the purpose of the advisory group.

2. Ask students to think about the rules needed for a group to be successful. These rules could also be expectations people have for one another if they are on the same team. Brainstorm a list of possible rules, listing them on the chalkboard.

3. Have the group agree on three to five rules.

   Sample Rules

   Respect the rights and feelings of others (no put-downs).

   Be a good listener.

   What is said in the room stays in the room (confidentiality).

   Everyone should participate and take turns sharing.

4. Make a poster with the final set of rules that your group develops and post it in your room. Review these rules on a regular basis.

The Name Game

Purpose   To help students learn the names of each group member

Materials   None

Procedure
1. Have students sit in a circle. Tell them you are all going on a picnic. Ask the person to your left to specify one item to bring along. That item must start with the first letter of the person's name. For example: "My name is David, and I am going to bring dill pickles" or "My name is Sharon, and I am going to bring slaw."

2. The next person must repeat everything the first person said and add his or her own name and picnic item. The third person must repeat the first and second persons' names and items and add to them, and so forth.

Variations
1. You may change the picnic idea to other things—for example, the circus, a birthday party, shopping, or school.

2. Geography teachers may want to challenge their students by asking them to use a map to find a city, town, or country beginning with the same letter as their name. For example: "My name is Susan, and I am traveling to Spokane" or "My name is Henry, and I am traveling to Helsinki." You could do this once within the United States and again outside the United States.

3. Ask students to form a circle. Give one group member a ball. This person says his or her name then says someone else's name in the circle and tosses the ball to him or her. After everyone has tossed the ball, see if anyone can go around the circle and state everyone's name.

Find Someone Who . . .

Purpose   To help participants learn other group members' names and something about them

Materials   Find Someone Treasure Hunt Form (Handout 2)
Human Bingo Card (Handout 3)

Procedure   1. Distribute copies of the Find Someone Treasure Hunt Form (Handout 2). Have students circulate around the room and collect signatures for 10 minutes. When the time is up, ask them to return to their seats.

2. Have students sit in a circle. Select three to five statements from the handout, then ask students who signed their names for specific responses. For example: "What book did you read?" "What team did you play on?"

3. Encourage students to continue meeting and greeting one another. Say, "I hope you have managed to introduce yourself to someone you did not previously know."

Variation   Use the Human Bingo Card (Handout 3).

Handout 2

FIND SOMEONE TREASURE HUNT FORM

Directions: Have a different person sign each line. Be sure the person can honestly sign his or her name to the statement.

I use mouthwash regularly. _____

I have traveled outside the United States. _____

I was born over 1,000 miles from here. _____

I cry at movies or watching TV sometimes. _____

I believe in equal rights for women. _____

I refuse to walk under a ladder. _____

I like classical music. _____

I have used an outhouse. _____

I have read a book in the last month. _____

I play a musical instrument. _____

I speak a foreign language. _____

I played on a summer sports team. _____

I sang in church. _____

I am allergic to something. _____

I hope to keep a neat locker. _____

HUMAN BINGO CARD

Directions: In each square, get the signature of a different person if the statement is true for them. Try to get a signature in each square. If all squares are filled, get additional signatures in each box.

Likes eggs	Cat lover	Has size 7 shoes
Reads the newspaper	Likes to dance	Likes camping
Watches stars	Swam in the ocean	Plays piano

Who Am I?

Purpose   To help students get to know one another better

Materials   Index cards and pencils
Chalkboard

Procedure   1. Give an index card and pencil to each student. On the chalkboard write the following items:

Number of people in your family

Something you do for fun

Something you dislike doing

A recent event that was new or good for you

Hobbies

2. Ask each student to write a response to these five items on the card. Be sure to fill out a card for yourself. Collect the cards.

3. Read each card to the class and have the group try to guess who is being described. After a few guesses, ask the person who wrote the card to identify himself or herself. Continue until everyone has been identified.

Variation   For a Halloween bulletin board activity, ask students to cut out a ghost shape from a white sheet of paper. They can then write the information about themselves on the front, with their names on the back. Make a black background for the bulletin board with "WHOOOO AM I???" posted at the top. Let students guess.

What We Enjoy

Purpose To encourage the group to work together and share some of the things they enjoy

Materials Chalkboard
Paper and pencil for each group

Procedure 1. Write the following on the chalkboard:

What We Enjoy . . .

TV show

Movie

Singing group

Food

Dessert

Radio station

Sport

Car

Book

School subject

2. Divide the class into groups of three or four students each and have each group come up with a group decision on what they enjoy in each category.

3. Have each group share their responses with the whole class. Share your own responses as well.

Variations 1. For a Thanksgiving Day activity, ask students to think of two things they are thankful for. In the smaller groups, encourage them to find at least three things everyone has in common.

2. Create a bulletin board to display groups' responses for each category. Give each group a sheet of construction paper to write or draw their responses.

Name Your Group

Purpose To develop group cohesion and encourage team building

Materials Poster board and markers

Procedure NOTE: This activity uses the brainstorming technique described in the Introduction.

1. Develop a list by brainstorming ideas about what it means to be a team.

2. Discuss how each person plays an important part on any team. Stress that we all have something to contribute.

3. Discuss some well-known team (such as athletic teams, businesses, or organizations) and what names and slogans they use to represent themselves.

4. Brainstorm names that might be used to describe your group and what your motto or slogan could be.

5. After some discussion, try to reach an agreement on a group name.

6. Have students submit designs for a logo with a slogan that follows the selected name.

7. Put the name, logo, and slogan on poster board. Display the poster in your room and/or in the hallway.

Variations 1. Have your group write a poem, song, or rap that describes the group members.

2. Take a photo of the group and place it on your poster.

3. Design and make buttons for your group.

4. Make a banner for the hallway with the group name, logo, and slogan.

Mural of Expressions

Purpose   To encourage students to express their ideas and feelings on a variety of topics in a nonthreatening way

Materials   Large piece of construction paper or tag board
Markers

Procedure   1. Mount the paper over a section of chalkboard or the wall, or use it to cover a tabletop. Put a sentence stem at the top of the paper. For example:

What I like about school is . . .

Friendship means . . .

I would like our group to have . . .

It's tough being a kid because . . .

Something that bugs me is . . .

Something I like to do on Saturday is . . .

2. Encourage students to express themselves freely on the topic chosen. You might wish to express your "teacher opinion" once the mural is completed. A few basic ground rules might be that everyone contributes at least once and nothing may be written that makes fun of another person.

3. After most of the students have contributed, conduct a class discussion focusing on the topic of the mural.

Variations   1. Invite a group of students to write an article on the mural topic for the school newspaper or newsletter.

2. Use the mural for current events. Encourage students to bring in pictures from a newspaper or magazine and tape them to the mural. Students would then be free to write their ideas or thoughts about any of the pictures.

Teacher Interview

Purpose To help students become better acquainted with their teacher

Materials Chalkboard

Procedure 1. Jot down 5 to 10 words on the board about yourself. These words might concern travel, sports, animals, adventure, books, risks, and so forth.

2. Ask students to pick a word and ask questions about it so that they find out more information about you as a person.

3. Invite students to ask other interviewing questions so that they might come to know you better. Agree that you may pass on any item.

4. After sharing some of your interests and life experiences with your students, ask students to complete the following sentence stems:

I learned that . . .

I was surprised that . . .

I wonder . . .

What I have in common with my teacher is . . .

Variations 1. If some students seem interested in sharing information about themselves with the class as you have, let them become the focus person.

2. Have students write an article about you for the school newspaper or newsletter.

3. Invite another member of the school for a similar interview. This might be the custodian, secretary, social worker, and so on.

Scavenger Hunt

Purpose To encourage students to communicate and work together as a group

Materials Paper bags and list of collectibles for each group

Procedure 1. Divide the group into small cooperative learning teams. Allow approximately four students to work per group. These should be students who have not previously worked together.

2. Have the larger group brainstorm a list of objects we come across on a daily basis.

List of Collectibles

Something brown

Nine short sticks

Something soft

Eleven tiny stones

Something prickly

Evidence of pollution

Five bottle caps or pop tops

A map

A feather

Fruit

Needles from a pine tree

Something homemade

Something manufactured

Something shiny

20 feet of string

3. Instruct the small groups to collaborate in collecting these "treasures" for the next group session. The team that brings in the most of the selected items is the top team.

Variation Follow up this activity by having the teams take all the collected items and turn them into a collage, mobile, or sculpture.

You + Me = Us

Purpose To compare and contrast, in a friendly way, what group members have in common

Materials Paper and pencils

Procedure 1. Have students partner up with someone they have not previously worked with. You may need to include yourself if there is an odd number of group members.

2. Show students a Venn diagram such as the following example.

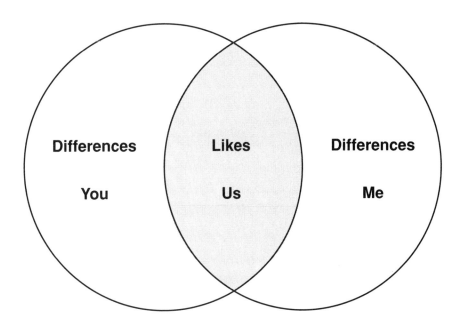

3. Ask students to think of things that they like or that are important to them. Have them discuss their list with their partners and find out what their differences and similarities are.

4. Have partners develop their own Venn diagram and share it with the larger group. See which pair can come up with the most similarities and differences.

Variations 1. Post all the diagrams around the room and discuss what common ground all people have.

2. Invite a student to tally all the things each pair had in common.

I Am Most Like . . .

Purpose   To encourage students to compare and contrast themselves to other things in the world

Materials   None

Procedure   1. Have students sit in a circle. Ask students to think about themselves by answering a number of questions and explaining why. Select several of the following questions for your group.

What plant are you most like?

What animal are you most like?

What cartoon character are you most like?

What vegetable are you most like?

What store in the mall are you most like?

What mode of transportation are you most like?

What piece of furniture are you most like?

What kind of car are you most like?

What candy or dessert are you most like?

What TV personality are you most like?

What fruit are you most like?

What sport are you most like?

2. Either divide into smaller groups and have students discuss their answers or discuss answers in the larger group. (In the larger group, fewer people might answer each question.)

Variations   1. Use a different question each day as a conversation starter and group warm-up activity.

2. Have students draw their answers, then display the drawings on a poster or bulletin board.

UNIT TWO

School Success

I wanted to convince you that you must learn to make every act count,
since you are going to be here for only a short while, in fact,
too short for witnessing all the marvels of it.

Carlos Castañeda, *Journey to Ixtlan*

Overview

A major part of a teenager's life is spent at school. School is a job, and if the teenager's performance is a good quality one, he or she will experience less stress and a greater sense of self-worth. A variety of skills are needed for successful school performance.

This unit begins with activities to help students learn about school rules, resources within the building, and the various adults who are there to help. Thinking about school rules as "life rules" (to be prompt, prepared, involved, and respectful) helps students generalize these rules to the world of work. Thinking about student rights and responsibilities helps promote fairness and respect among students and between students and teachers.

One of the most frequent concerns of parents and teachers of students this age is disorganization. The students' lockers are a mess, they lose assignments, and they are never sure what their homework is or when it is due. Thus, activities are included to teach and reinforce organizational skills as responsible behavior. Students will become more self-reliant and self-sufficient when they master good organizational skills.

A final topic of the activities in this unit concerns self-evaluation and goal setting. What we expect of ourselves and what others expect of us often determine our performance. Students must see school as important and themselves as capable before they can perform successfully. Students can learn to develop a sense of quality and recognize efforts and accomplishment. Self-evaluation and goal setting helps students become responsible for their own learning and increases self-motivation. When students become their own best experts, they become involved in a new way in the educational process.

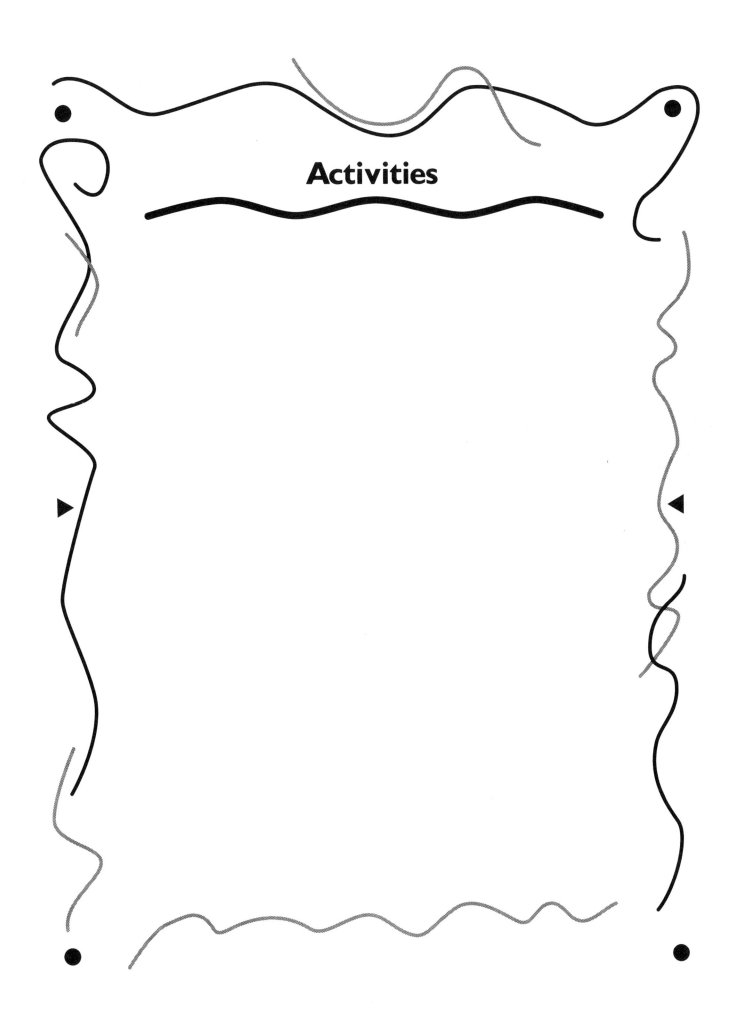

Activities

Know Your School

Purpose To help students learn and understand correct school procedures and rules

Materials A copy of the school's student handbook for at least every two students
Know Your School (Handout 4)

Procedure 1. Read and review the student handbook with students. Discuss with them why rules and regulations are necessary. You may want to point out that most of these rules are consistent with those they have had in the past. Give special attention to rules that are unique to your building.

2. Divide the group into smaller groups of three to four students each. Distribute copies of the Know Your School form (Handout 4).

3. Have students work cooperatively to find the answers to the questions in the handbook. (Adapt the handout as necessary to follow your own school rules.)

Variations 1. Use the handout as an individual competency test. The person in charge of discipline in your building could keep them on file for future reference. If individual students have a problem, the disciplinarian can remind them of the test.

2. Turn this activity into a board game and keep it in the school library for all to play.

Handout 4

KNOW YOUR SCHOOL

Directions: Find out the answers to the following questions.

1. What do I do when I am late to school?

2. How many times can I be late to school before I start receiving detentions?

3. Where do I serve after school detentions?

4. If I need to leave school for a doctor's appointment, what arrangements do I need to make?

5. I lost my book. Now what do I do?

6. The lock on my locker is broken. Whom do I tell?

7. What do I do if another student is threatening me?

8. How do I make an appointment with the school counselor or social worker?

9. List three behaviors that should be practiced in the hallway.

10. Write three items that are not to be brought to school.

11. Define "grossly unacceptable behaviors" for which a person might be suspended from school.

School Bingo

Purpose To provide the opportunity for students to meet the adults working in their school

Materials Chalkboard
Paper and pencils

Procedure 1. Brainstorm with your group the job titles of the different adults working in your school. Write these titles on the chalkboard.

2. Have each student fold a piece of paper into eight sections. At the top of each of the eight sections, have the students write a different job title. For example:

custodian	hall monitor
cook	art teacher
administrator	PE teacher
counselor	librarian
track coach	foreign language teacher

3. Review with students the appropriate way to greet a stranger. You can have the school social worker or counselor come in to assist in this demonstration. Explain to the students that, in each square, they are to get the signature of a person who fits the job title.

4. When students next come to class, discuss their experiences in getting the sheet filled in.

School Trivia

Purpose To encourage students to learn special information about their school

Materials None

Procedure 1. Develop a list of school trivia questions, or have students devise a list. For example:

How many ceiling tiles are in Room 110?

What year was our school built?

Our principal's birthday is _____.

The teacher who has taught in our building the longest is _____.

The library has _____ books.

The current enrollment of our building is _____.

How many telephones are there in our building?

How many steps must you climb to get to the second floor?

What percentage of students get to school by bus?

What is the most expensive text book to lose?

2. Have students form groups of three to four to determine the answers to the trivia questions. Give the groups a week to collect the information.

3. During the next group time, verify the information and discuss students' experiences getting it.

Variations 1. Include the information in the school newsletter or newspaper.

2. Have students develop additional trivia questions and challenge other groups.

3. Use "experts" on this information as tour guides for the building during open house. Parents and visitors will be highly impressed by the knowledge these students can share.

Your School As You See It

Purpose   To give students an opportunity to understand their school environment better and to discuss their feelings about school

Materials   Chalkboard

Procedure   NOTE: Even though students experience and are a part of the school culture, they may not be aware of how differently other individuals within the school perceive the environment. This activity will examine some of the reasons for these differences, looking specifically at the various groups in your school.

1. Either in the large group or small groups, have students brainstorm positives and negatives about their school. Write these ideas on the chalkboard for all members of the group to see.

2. Discuss how some members may find an item to be a positive, whereas other students may see that same thing as a negative. You may want to ask students if they see a cup of water as half full or half empty.

3. Discuss the following topics, as appropriate:

   Do you think everyone at school is treated fairly?

   Does everyone have the same experiences and feelings about school?

   Why are some students' experiences so different from others'?

   Do you think teachers and principals expect certain students to have a difficult time at school? What groups and why?

   Do you think schools are prejudiced toward certain groups of students who behave differently, dress differently, or who don't learn so easily? Are there any other groups like these that you can think of?

Variations   1. Have the class develop a list of constructive suggestions that could be shared with staff members to support diversity and create a school climate where all students can have good experiences.

2. Encourage cultural awareness by arranging for activities or displays that celebrate diversity.

3. Design a cultural awareness week. Celebrate by inviting members of the community with different ethnic backgrounds to present information on their heritage. These presenters might discuss food, dance, geography, culture, clothing, economics, festivals, and so forth.

Rights and Responsibilities

Purpose To teach students about their rights and responsibilities in the classroom and school

Materials Chalkboard

Procedure 1. Ask the group what rights they have at school. List them on the chalkboard.

2. Ask the group what responsibilities they have if these rights are not to be violated. Document the responses on the board. See how many different examples students can give.

3. Share with students the following rights and responsibilities.

Rights	Responsibilities
To be treated with kindness: No one will tease you or insult you.	To treat others as you want to be treated.
To be yourself: No one will treat you unfairly due to looks, abilities, or gender.	To allow others to be themselves.
To be safe: No one will threaten you, bully you, or damage your property.	To allow others to feel safe.
To be heard: No one will yell at you, and your opinions will be considered.	To listen and let others be heard.
To learn about yourself: You are free to express your feelings and opinions without being criticized.	To allow others to learn and express their ideas.

4. Discuss why some students do not act in a responsible way at school.

5. Debate whether these rights and responsibilities are fair.

6. Determine which of these responsibilities might be hardest to follow.

Variations 1. Have students investigate what the school board policy is for students' rights and responsibilities. See how it compares to your list.

2. Change the topic to teachers' or parents' rights and responsibilities.

3. Have students make a permanent poster of the rights and responsibilities list for display.

Classroom Rules Prepare Us for Life

Purpose   To understand rules teachers use in the classroom and how they help students prepare for life

Materials   Chalkboard
Life Rules: Ways to Be (Handout 5)

Procedure
1. Write the following words on the chalkboard: *prompt, prepared, involved,* and *respectful.* Have students try to apply each word to a classroom situation.

2. Distribute copies of Life Rules: Ways to Be (Handout 5). Talk about any ideas on the handout that have not already been discussed.

3. Discuss with students how school would be different if everyone followed these rules. Ask whether it is possible for all of these rules to be followed all the time. Why or why not?

4. Ask students to predict how these same rules apply to life outside of school. For instance, how are these rules a part of piano lessons? Do they apply to basketball or football players?

5. Divide students into small groups and have them brainstorm how many ways they can apply these rules to their lives outside of school.

Variations
1. Have students predict how these life rules will affect each of them in the future.

2. Ask students to list as many careers as they can in 5 minutes. Go through the list, one by one, and ask how not following one of the life rules would make success in that career impossible. For example:

   What happens when the fire fighter is not prompt?

   How could a restaurant survive without preparation?

   What might happen if a doctor decides not to be involved?

   What might happen if a teacher is not respectful?

LIFE RULES: WAYS TO BE

Be Prompt

I am in my seat when the bell rings.

I turn in my work on time.

I am ready to learn.

Be Prepared

I bring my materials to class.

I complete my class assignments.

I turn in my homework.

Be Involved

I listen to my teachers and classmates.

I answer questions when called on.

I work with my team members in group assignments.

I do quality work.

Be Respectful

I sit quietly and pay attention.

I speak politely to teachers and students.

I keep my hands and feet to myself.

I take care of school property.

I allow others their opinions and beliefs.

Study Tips

Purpose   To provide suggestions for how to study effectively

Materials   Chalkboard

Procedure   1. Have students share different study tips. Jot these down on the chalkboard as statements the students can say to themselves to help keep a positive attitude and improve their performance. For example:

Keeping a positive attitude will help me to be more successful.

Being aware of my limits and strengths will help me to avoid problems and focus on the good.

Using my assignment sheet will help keep me organized.

Budgeting my time wisely will keep me prepared daily.

The place I study is free of distractions.

Establishing a routine is helpful.

Knowing where to get help when I need it is important.

Listening in class is crucial.

Carrying an organized notebook is a must.

Choosing the right study partners is important.

Taking good notes and quizzing myself often will improve my grades.

Keeping myself healthy is necessary.

2. Discuss the pros and cons of the various ideas. If individual students verbalize why a specific technique may not work for them, have the others brainstorm a solution to these students' problems.

Variation   Have a student type the list of study ideas. Make enough copies so each person can keep one in the front of his or her notebook. Have students occasionally refer to this list to check on how they are doing.

Monthly Planning

Purpose   To assist students in becoming more organized both at school and at home

Materials   Monthly Calendar (Handout 6)

Procedure   NOTE: This activity can be done on a monthly basis to share special school information. Inform other teachers that the monthly calendars exist so they can make additions.

1. Ask students the following questions:

   In what class do you have the most homework?

   In what class do you have the most tests?

   Which subject is the hardest for you?

   Which subject is the easiest for you?

   How much time do you study each night?

   How much time do you play or watch TV each night?

2. Tell students that everyone needs to assess his or her own needs: Different classes have different requirements. Life at home has responsibilities. Just as important is "R and R"—rest and relaxation.

3. Explain that most adults keep an appointment book or some type of calendar to stay organized. Students are now at a point where they too need to keep track of all their important activities.

4. Distribute copies of the Monthly Calendar (Handout 6). Inform students of events occurring for that particular month (dances, plays, concerts, tests, project deadlines, and so on), then have them write these on their individual calendars.

5. Next have students list their personal activities (for example, piano lessons, karate lessons, basketball practices and games, when library books are due, friends' and family members' birthdays).

Variation   Keep one master calendar of school events in the classroom.

Handout 6

MONTHLY CALENDAR

Month _____

Monday	Tuesday	Wednesday	Thursday	Friday	Weekend
☐	☐	☐	☐	☐	☐
☐	☐	☐	☐	☐	☐
☐	☐	☐	☐	☐	☐
☐	☐	☐	☐	☐	☐
☐	☐	☐	☐	☐	☐

Asking for Help

Purpose To help students be able to find and ask for help

Materials None

Procedure
1. Discuss the variety of situations students may encounter at school in which they might need assistance.

2. Next list all the people in the school who could be helpful. These might include teachers, custodians, librarians, parent volunteers, lunchroom supervisors, and so forth.

3. Explain that resources are available all around you and that if there are things you don't understand, you should find the best person in order to get help.

4. Discuss the following situations. Ask where students might get help in each situation.

   You lost your coat.

   Another student bugs you on the bus.

   You forget your locker combination.

   Your locker won't open.

   You come to school late.

   You have problems with a teacher.

   Your materials for a class project are stolen.

   A friend needs a winter coat, but his or her parents don't have the money.

   You don't know how to write a term paper.

   Your PE clothes are missing.

Who's Got the Time?

Purpose   To help students become aware of how they use their time and evaluate whether they might be able to use it more wisely

Materials   Paper and pencils

Procedure   1. Ask students to brainstorm a list of daily activities that take up their time (for example, going to school, watching TV, talking on the phone, doing chores, sleeping, eating, grooming, talking to parents).

2. Go back through the list and ask students to estimate how much time they spend at each activity each day.

3. Have students design a personal graph showing how they choose to spend their time. This can be a bar or pie graph. For example:

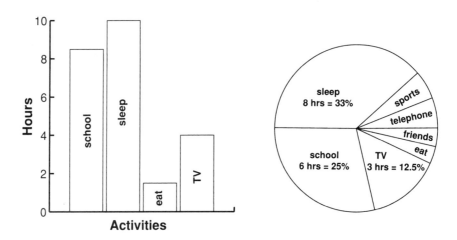

4. After the graphs are complete, have students share them with the group. Ask students how they might change the way they spend their time. What would they like to be spending more time doing? Less time doing?

Variations   1. Ask students to do the same assignment for one of their parents. Have them share these charts and any responses from parents with the class.

2. Challenge students to give up all electronic entertainment (TV, video games, stereo, Walkman, and so forth) for a week or more to see how their lives will change. Discuss the change.

Wellness and Learning

Purpose   To encourage students to draw a connection between their physical health and school performance

Materials   None

Procedure   1. Ask students if they ever come to school not feeling very well. If they are not sick, ask them for some of the reasons for not feeling well (for example, not enough sleep, no breakfast, didn't shower).

2. Explain that "wellness" means both physical and mental health. Wellness means that you have the following:

   Plenty of sleep

   Plenty of exercise

   Time to relax

   Healthy meals

   Regular check-ups

   Good grooming and hygiene

3. Ask students to think about this list and share an area where they think they are doing well. Have them share an area where they could use some improvement.

Variations   1. Ask students to record the amount of junk food, sweets, and soda pop they consume for a week. Have them calculate the amount of money they spend on such items. Challenge the students to go for a week without junk food, sweets, or soda pop.

2. Have students record their sleep patterns. Compare results and discuss.

Organization Is the Key

Purpose   To create ways for students to become more organized

Materials   Weekly Assignment Sheet (Handout 7)
Tips for Being Organized (Handout 8)

Procedure   1. Tell students there are lots of ways to organize your materials. The system you choose works only if you use it. Brainstorm a list of ideas of ways to be organized.

2. Discuss the most important ideas and talk about materials students can use to help themselves get organized. For example:

Individual notebooks for each class

Folders with pockets for each class (pockets are a great place to keep returned papers)

A trapper or binder to keep everything in

Plenty of sharpened pencils with erasers

3. Discuss ways to keep track of assignments:

Have a calendar or appointment book.

Use a weekly assignment sheet (see Handout 7).

Try keeping a special page in your notebook.

4. Encourage students to avoid lines such as these:

I know I have it someplace.

I crammed it in my locker and can't find it.

I folded it up, and I thought I put it in my book.

I left it at home.

5. Read and discuss Tips for Being Organized (Handout 8).

Variations   1. Have a specific day each month for locker and binder clean outs. Notify the custodian so extra trash cans will be in the hallway.

2. Offer monthly incentives to students who hand in all assignments, projects, and parent-teacher notes on time. These may include free library time, free computer time, game time, a free water break, a pencil, and so on.

3. Design a bulletin board with the theme "Organization Is the Key." Cut keys out of construction paper and write on them the various tips to being organized. This will help remind everyone who passes through the room.

Handout 7

WEEKLY ASSIGNMENT SHEET   From ——— to ——— Name ———

Class	Monday	Tuesday	Wednesday	Thursday	Friday

ACTIVITY 24

Handout 8

TIPS FOR BEING ORGANIZED

Be Prepared for Class

1. Be prepared for every class. Bring book, pencil or pen, paper, notebook, and assignment book to each class.

2. Clear your desk—put books on the floor. It is easier to do your work with a clear desk.

3. Don't be late for class, and be ready to start when class starts. Important instructions are given at the beginning of the class, so try not to visit your locker between each class.

4. Be organized. Keep papers filed for each class in a folder or notebook.

5. Always bring required assignments or homework to class.

Be Prepared to Study

1. Have a well-lighted place away from distractions.

2. Do not leave homework until the last minute. Plan a time when you are ready and alert to do quality work.

3. Do not leave your least favorite subjects to do last—do them first to get them out of the way.

Be Involved

1. Try not to miss class unless it is absolutely necessary. Information presented in class is most easily learned if you are there and paying attention. Your attendance and attention will mean less homework.

2. If you miss a test or quiz, make it up as soon as possible. The longer you wait, the less information you will remember.

3. If you are falling behind or have questions, meet with the teacher out of class either after school or at lunch—whenever the teacher is willing to meet.

Individual Goal Setting

Purpose   To encourage students to identify and set goals for themselves

Materials   Index cards
Grade Yourself (Handout 9)
Goals for My Next Report Card (Handout 10)

Procedure   1. Discuss with students the importance of goal setting: Goals are like a map. They give us direction and a point from which we can evaluate our progress. Discuss how hard it is to set goals that give us direction in life. Discuss the self-talk "How can I fail if I have no direction?"

2. Distribute the Grade Yourself worksheet (Handout 9). Have students take a few minutes and fill out both parts of the sheet. Discuss the relationship of the grades students received in various subjects and how they graded themselves on the items listed on the sheet. Have students share some of their responses to the sentence completions.

3. Distribute Goals for My Next Report Card (Handout 10). Give students a few minutes to complete both parts of the form. Ask students to share some of the things they are going to do to accomplish their goals. Ask students to post this sheet in their lockers to be a reminder and give them direction.

Variations   1. Copy students' Goals for My Next Report Card sheets (Handout 10) and save these until the end of the next grading period. Pass them back so students can see how they did at accomplishing their goals.

2. Have students write other goals on index cards. These goals can concern anything from friends and family to fitness. Discuss how setting goals is like making New Year's resolutions. Discuss ways students can think of to keep their resolutions.

Handout 9

GRADE YOURSELF

Part I

Directions: Your teachers evaluated you during the last grading period. Now you get a chance to evaluate yourself. Circle the grade you would honestly give yourself.

1. My notebook is organized and I use an assignment sheet.

     A   B   C   D   F

2. I come to class prepared with pencil, paper, books, and so on.

     A   B   C   D   F

3. I pay attention in class and listen.

     A   B   C   D   F

4. I complete my homework on time.

     A   B   C   D   F

5. My work in school is quality work.

     A   B   C   D   F

6. I work well cooperatively with my peers.

     A   B   C   D   F

Part II

Directions: Now complete these sentences about your last report card.

1. The first thing that comes to mind about my last report card is _____

   _____.

2. I think the grades on my report card were _____.

3. I need to ask for more help in _____.

4. In order to get better grades I need to _____

   _____.

5. School would be more fun if I would _____

   _____.

GOALS FOR MY NEXT REPORT CARD

Part I

Directions: Fill out the courses you are taking, the grade you received in the past, and the grade you hope to receive in the future.

Courses	Grade received	Grade I plan to receive
1		
2		
3		
4		
5		
6		
7		

Part II

Directions: Think of two classes you would especially like to focus on. Think of at least two things you will need to do differently to achieve the grade you set as your goal.

Class _____ Goal _____

Two things I need to do in order to accomplish this goal:

1. _____

2. _____

Class _____ Goal _____

Two things I need to do in order to accomplish this goal:

1. _____

2. _____

ACTIVITY 26

Thank-You Notes

Purpose To help students learn to appreciate what others have done for them and express that gratitude in written form

Materials Paper or note cards

Procedure 1. Explain to students that for many people expressing gratitude is difficult: Often you just can't come up with the best words to fit the situation. It's not that you aren't appreciative of all the little and big things friends, relatives, and teachers do for you. For example:

You felt really grateful when a friend loaned you a dollar to buy lunch the other day.

Your English teacher shared some extra time to help you organize your report.

When you forgot your book bag the bus driver returned it to the school.

2. Ask students what people they think deserve their special thanks:

Librarian

Custodian

Secretary

School counselor

Nurse

Speech teacher

Yearbook sponsor

Administrator

Relative

Friend

3. Ask each student to do four thank-you notes: two for teachers, one for a relative, and one for a friend. Distribute note cards or have students fold a sheet of paper into quarters and make their own notes.

4. After students are finished, ask them how this activity made them feel. During the next group, see what responses they got from their notes.

Variations   1. Have students write thank-you notes for inclusion in the school newsletter or newspaper.

2. Encourage students to write a thank-you poem, song, or rap for a special person at school.

3. Have students make a videotape for a particular staff member thanking him or her for a fine job. Send the videotape home with the staff member.

Challenging School Situations

Purpose   To help students work cooperatively in small groups, practicing pro-social skills and a positive attitude toward challenging school situations

Materials   Index cards (prepared beforehand with a role-play situation written on each)

Procedure   1. Discuss tough situations that occur at school. Explain how some of these situations can create stress for some people.

2. Divide students into small groups. Pass out three index cards to each group, on each of which you have written a separate role-play situation. For example:

A teacher treats you in a way you don't like.

You get a detention that you feel is unfair.

You don't have enough lunch money.

You did the wrong page for your math homework.

You have to tell the librarian that you can't find your library book.

You need to use the telephone in the office.

You can't dress out for PE today because _____.

You need to set up an appointment with the school counselor.

You want to introduce yourself to a new student at school.

You weren't here yesterday, and you need to find out the correct procedure for clearing your absence and getting the work you missed.

You can't get your locker open.

You need to give someone directions to get to the gym.

3. Ask the groups to act out the role-play situations on their cards, demonstrating a negative outcome and a positive outcome for each one. Tell students that all members are to be an active part of the role-play. You may wish to assign roles, including the role of director for each role-play, or members may draw their roles out of a hat.

4. After each pair of role-plays, discuss why in one demonstration the situation had a negative outcome and in the other the situation had a positive outcome.

Variation   Have students perform their role-plays for other groups or videotape them for future viewing. Videotapes may be helpful to incoming students.

Preparing for Next Year

Purpose To encourage a smooth transition from one grade level to another

Materials None

Procedure NOTE: This activity should be done at the end of the school year.

1. In small groups, have students develop questions they have for the coming school year. Invite to your classroom a panel of teachers and/or students a grade level ahead to address the students' questions. Give special attention to rules and regulations that will change in the coming school year.

2. Take the students on a walk to visit their future classrooms. (This may help relieve stress some may feel over the summer vacation.)

3. Optional: Provide two lists, one of books students could read during the vacation in preparation for the next grade and the other of supplies they will need to obtain for the coming school year.

Variation On April 1, have teachers at the next grade level swap classrooms with the teachers at the grade level below to meet and work with their next year's students. This has an added bonus because the older students get to revisit their former teachers.

Words for Discussion

COOPERATION

Personalize   Give an example of a time you had to cooperate to accomplish a task.

How do you feel when you cooperate with others?

How do you feel when you compete with others?

Which way works best for you? When and why?

What role (leader, follower, joker, critic, other) do you play in a cooperative group situation?

Define   Cooperation = Joint action or effort for mutual benefit.

Challenge   Make two suggestions that would help a learning group or team be more successful.

Why might you compete in some situations and cooperate in others?

LEADERSHIP

Personalize   In what ways would you act differently if you were a celebrity and had a fan club of younger kids who idolized you and tried to copy everything you did?

Think of the leaders in your peer group. What are some of their traits?

How do people become leaders? Are leaders born or made?

Define   Leadership = The ability to influence, control, or direct others.

Challenge   Would you like to be more of a leader?

What skills would you have to develop to assume a leadership role?

How can you have a positive influence over others without being a leader?

SUCCESS

Personalize Give an example of a time you experienced success.

How did you feel before your successful experience?

How do you feel when friends and family members succeed?

Why is it important to you to be successful?

Who in your eyes is the most successful person you know?

Define Success = A favorable result, wished-for ending, or good fortune.

Challenge Determine what, in the next 2 weeks, you would like to be successful doing. How do you plan on gaining that success? What happens when you are not successful at something? What do you do then?

How can you help others who may not always be successful?

AUTHORITY

Personalize Whom do you consider a person in authority?

What has that person done to gain authority?

What do you have authority over?

Predict what would happen to our world if we had no authority figures.

Define Authority = The right to control, command, or make decisions; the power to enforce obedience; jurisdiction.

Challenge Would you like to have more authority?

What skills or knowledge do you need to gain authority?

How do you treat people in authority? Is that good or bad?

Do you need to change the way you treat people in authority? If so, how do you plan on doing that?

DISCIPLINE

Personalize In what situations do you need to discipline yourself? Is it hard or easy?

Do others ever need to discipline you? Why do they need to do that?

How do you react to others' efforts to discipline you?

Define Discipline = Training, especially training of the mind or character.

Challenge	As a group, develop suggestions to relieve discipline problems in your school. Take the ideas to the person in your building in charge of discipline.
	Keep a record in your notebook of times you have been disciplined.
	Investigate what causes discipline problems to occur in your life.

CONSEQUENCE

Personalize	What are some negative and positive consequences you have experienced?
	Is there any way of avoiding negative consequences?
	Are negative consequences necessary for a productive and healthy life?
Define	Consequence = Result or effect; outcome.
Challenge	Give yourself a consequence for a mistake you made.
	Think of a consequence you received that taught you responsibility.
	How should school or home give fair consequences that teach responsible behaviors?

EVALUATION

Personalize	Why is it important to evaluate your performance?
	Is it better to evaluate yourself or have someone else evaluate you?
	Are you more open to self-, peer, or teacher evaluation?
	After evaluation, do you attempt to make any changes?
Define	Evaluation = To estimate the worth or importance of something.
Challenge	Evaluate how your group is functioning. Include the positives and areas that need improvement.
	Evaluate your school performance. What are the positives and areas you plan to change?
	Evaluate other areas of the school or school functions (for example, the cafeteria, the outside of the building, school dances). To whom should you give your feedback?

SUPPORT

Personalize	Who are the people who give you support?
	When was the last time you provided support for someone?
	Share a time in which you needed support from someone else. Who supported you, and how did it make you feel to be supported?
	Do you prefer to give or receive support?

Define   Support = To give strength or courage to; keep up; help.

Challenge Give a member of the group support with a positive statement.

Show support to an important adult in your life. Bring back
to the next session what it was you did for that person.

FUTURE

Personalize Do you think the world will be a better or worse place 20 years from
now (environment, health, war, and so forth)? Why or why not?

What worries you most about the future?

How far in the future do you plan? Only today? Tomorrow?
Next week? Next year?

Define   Future = The time yet to come—tomorrow, next week, next month,
the rest of your life.

Challenge Think about where you will be and what you will be doing when you
are 25 years old. Job? Family? Location?

What will you have done about your worries of the future?

QUALITY

Personalize Give an example of a time you did a quality job or turned in
quality work.

How has working for quality helped you? Has it ever hurt you?

How do you recognize quality? What does it take to make a quality
product?

Define   Quality = Degree of excellence, relative goodness—your best efforts.

Challenge Evaluate your work in one of your classes. Is it good quality?
How can you help yourself do quality work?

Evaluate a relationship you have with a friend or family member.
How can you improve the quality of that relationship?

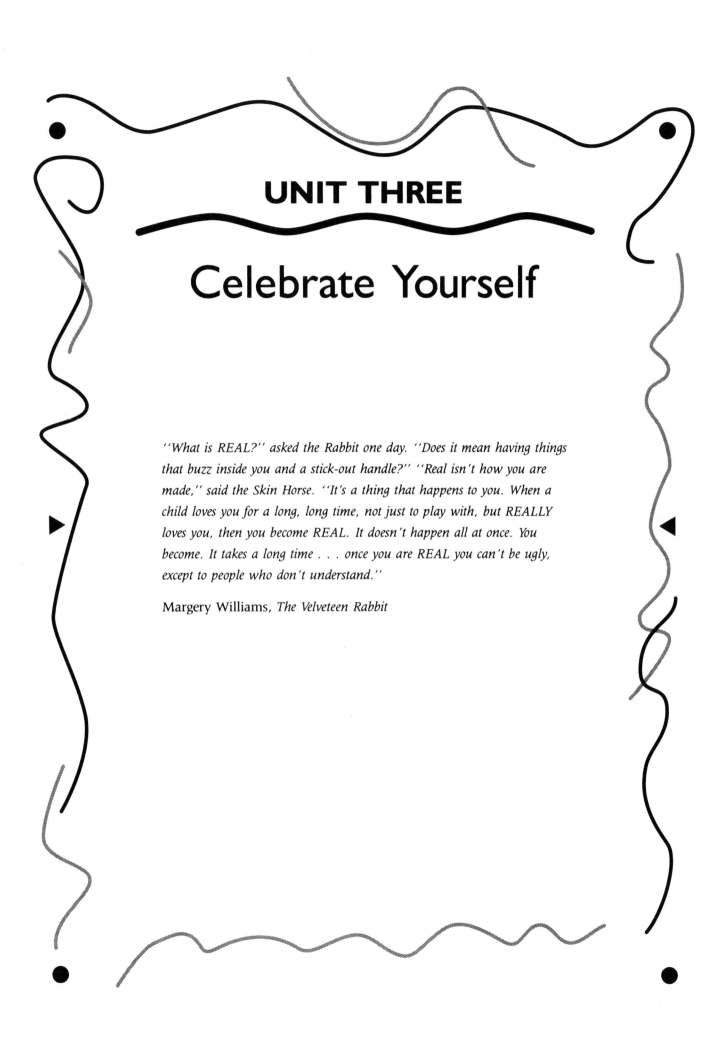

UNIT THREE

Celebrate Yourself

"What is REAL?" asked the Rabbit one day. "Does it mean having things that buzz inside you and a stick-out handle?" "Real isn't how you are made," said the Skin Horse. "It's a thing that happens to you. When a child loves you for a long, long time, not just to play with, but REALLY loves you, then you become REAL. It doesn't happen all at once. You become. It takes a long time . . . once you are REAL you can't be ugly, except to people who don't understand."

Margery Williams, *The Velveteen Rabbit*

Overview

The way in which we learn to think about ourselves influences all aspects of our lives—school performance, relationships, employment, and so on. At every stage of our lives, our self-concept influences how we perceive the world as well as how we feel, think, behave, and interact with others. How we learn to perceive ourselves is dependent on the culture we grow up in. The dominant culture in the United States focuses on individual achievement and expression. It appreciates "I-ness." Other cultures may define self more in terms of "we-ness"—for example, within the context of the family group—or in a more spiritual way.

Often we find ourselves chasing after rainbows (the hope of success, power, wealth, or the approval of others) that we think will make us happy. Surely, we tell ourselves, if we can just get beyond where we are, around the corner will be the pot of gold. We can search the world over and never achieve these ends. Or we may achieve some of these ends and still not be happy. Happiness does not come from material things or from other people. It cannot be bought. It is, like other dreams, totally personal and comes from within. That's often the last place we bother to look.

Looking within is what this unit's activities are all about. Everything we feel, think, and do is generated by what happens inside of us. Self-evaluation is the key to responsible and effective living. The activities presented here will help you and your students spend some time getting to know yourselves—your strengths, limitations, habits, fears, opinions, feelings, and goals. Improving relationships with ourselves improves our relationships with others.

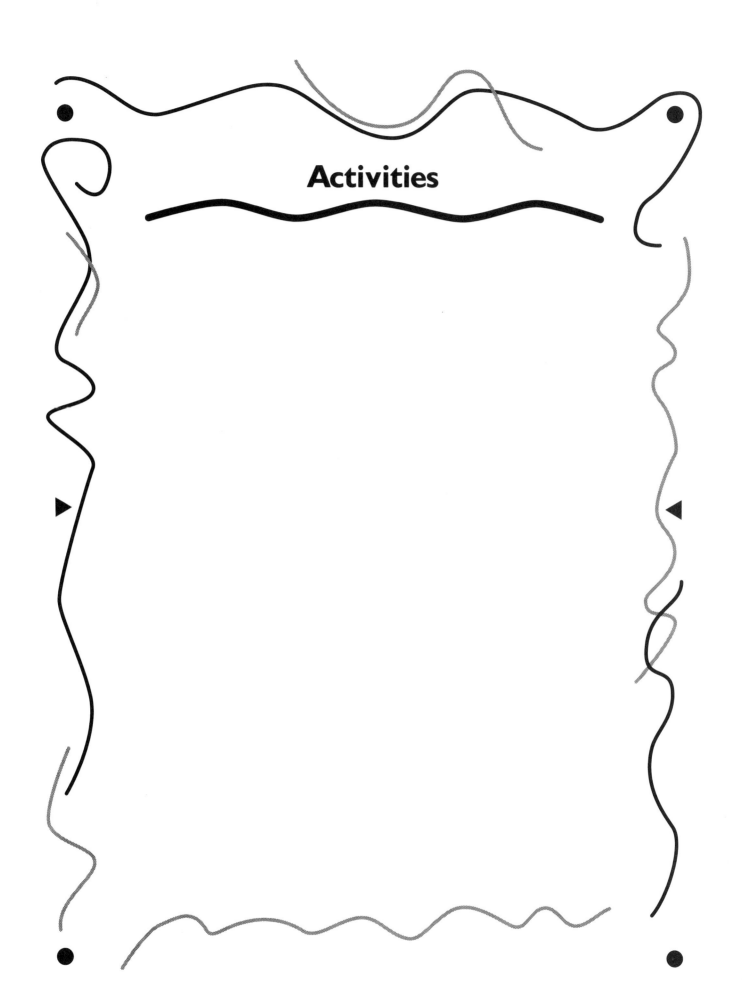

Activities

Yin and Yang

Purpose To encourage students to share their strengths and challenges

Materials Yin and Yang (Handout 11)

Procedure 1. Tell students that this activity will help them get to know one another better and recognize their own strengths and challenges (weaknesses).

2. Distribute the Yin and Yang drawing (Handout 11). Explain that the Yin and Yang is an old Chinese symbol for opposites—the good and bad, the dangers and opportunities of life. Point out that in every situation and in everyone's life there are pluses and minuses, good and bad.

3. Have each student think of two or three positive qualities or skills as well as two or three major challenges. Have each student draw or write these on the Yin and Yang symbol. For example:

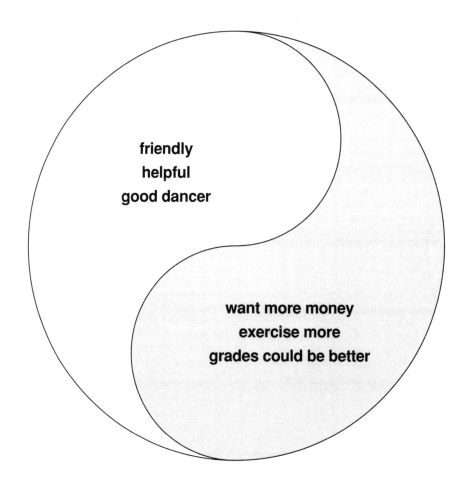

friendly
helpful
good dancer

want more money
exercise more
grades could be better

4. After students have completed their drawings, have them share with the group. Be sure to fill one out for yourself and share it as well.

5. Post the drawings on a classroom bulletin board.

Variation   Have each student design a personal coat of arms, including categories such as what I like to do, my family, something I value, and a place I have visited.

Handout II

YIN AND YANG

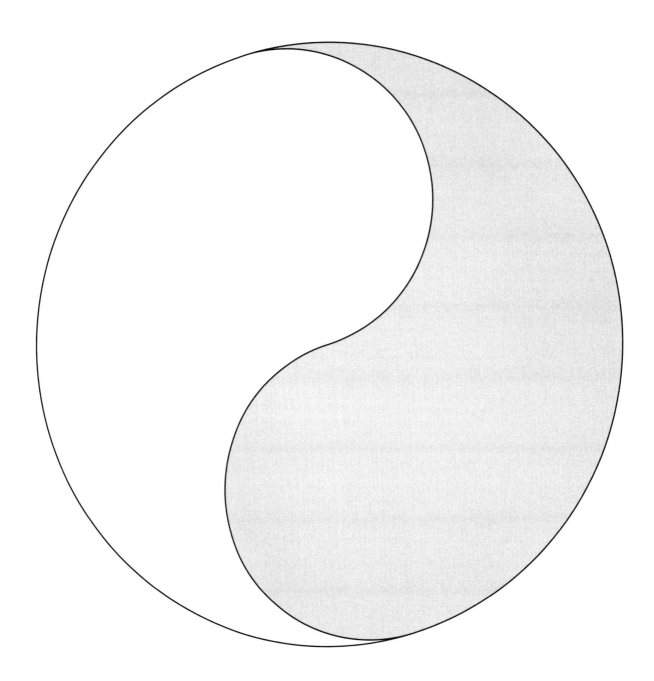

Take Home a Sack: Accepting Compliments

Purpose To learn to give and accept compliments

Materials Strips of paper and pencils
Lunch sacks

Procedure NOTE: Many children and adults have trouble accepting and giving compliments. Stress that students are to write nothing negative about anyone. You may want to give some examples of acceptable compliments. In addition, this activity must be done after students already know one another.

1. Divide the students into groups of six.

2. Give each group member six strips of paper and a lunch sack. Instruct each student to write his or her name on the sack.

3. Ask each student to write a positive statement or compliment for each person in his or her group and place it in that student's sack. Students should also write one positive statement about themselves and place it in their own sack.

4. Give the groups 10 minutes to write the compliments. Provide extra slips of paper for those who want to write more statements.

5. In the larger group, ask each student to share two of the statements placed in his or her bag. Discuss how students felt when others made positive statements and how it felt to write positive statements about themselves.

6. Students might want to tape these statements in their lockers to look at daily.

Variation Create a special sack for a teacher, student, volunteer parent, or another person around the school who deserves a kind word. This may be someone who would appreciate special recognition or who is moving or retiring.

Feelings Charades

Purpose   To familiarize students with a vocabulary that expresses feelings

Materials   Chalkboard
Index cards

Procedure

1. Brainstorm a list of feelings on the chalkboard. Have a student write each response on a separate index card. Be sure to have at least 25 cards. For example: *happy, excited, calm, capable, inspired, mellow, satisfied, worthy, proud, hurt, concerned, bored, angry, pressured, rejected, teased, miserable, and annoyed.*

2. Erase the board, then divide the class into two teams.

3. Shuffle the index cards. Have pairs of students come up, draw a card, and silently act out the feeling. Give fellow team members 30 seconds to guess the word.

4. Discuss how nonverbal communication can show how other people might feel.

Variations

1. Go back through the cards and ask students to describe times when they felt the various emotions.

2. Have the group try to make a list of 50 feeling words and give examples of situations in which someone felt that way.

3. Give everyone a feelings card and have them write a paragraph about that feeling.

4. Play the feelings charades game against another group.

5. Find pictures in newspapers and magazines portraying the various feelings. Discuss why these people have such feelings.

A Special Tribute to . . .

Purpose   To help students project into the future what they want to be known for and to encourage them to begin thinking about the direction they want their lives to take

Materials   Paper and pencils

Procedure   1. Tell students that there is going to be an evening honoring their retirement. They are to compose a tribute to themselves highlighting what they have achieved and what they will be remembered for.

2. Ask each student to write a paragraph saying how he or she will be introduced and honored.

3. Collect all the papers and read each to the group. Let the group guess who they think the person is who is being honored.

Variations   1. Role-play a special evening, with various members of the group taking turns talking about one student who is the honored guest.

2. Tell the students that each has won a Nobel Prize. Let them know that there are many categories for this award—science, literature, peace, and so forth. Ask them what Nobel Prize they might win and what they might have done to earn it.

3. Have students design cereal boxes with their picture on the front and a biographical sketch on the back.

4. Develop a student-of-the-week bulletin board. Have all the students put their names in a hat. Draw one name a week. The person whose name is chosen gets to design a bulletin board about himself or herself.

Personal Qualities

Purpose To help students identify and clarify what personal qualities are important to them and why

Materials Chalkboard
Paper and pencils

Procedure 1. List the following personal qualities on the chalkboard. Ask students to define the terms as you write them down.

Popularity

Uniqueness

Sensitivity

Athletic ability

Good looks

Sense of humor

Honesty

Intelligence

Helpfulness

Level-headedness

Creativity

Pride

2. Have students get into groups of four to five each and rank the qualities (from 1 to 12) in the order they think is most important in a close friend.

3. Have the groups come together and compare their rankings. Discuss why the rankings are the way they are.

Variation Encourage students to determine which of the 12 qualities are characteristic of people like Oprah Winfrey, Michael Jordan, Malcom X, Steve Martin, Sandra Day O'Connor, and so on. Discuss how these qualities helped these people be what they are today.

Self-Esteem Assessment

Purpose To help students define and assess their self-esteem

Materials None

Procedure 1. Explain to the students that we all have good days and not-so-good days. We also feel secure and competent in some life situations, but we avoid others. The degree to which we feel lovable and capable is a measure of our self-esteem.

2. Read the following items and ask students to think about themselves. Have them show thumbs up if a statement is usually true for them and thumbs down if it is mostly false.

I enjoy waking up in the morning.

I am usually in a good mood—day or night.

I like what I see in the mirror.

I enjoy being at school.

I have plenty of the good things in life.

I am an optimistic person.

I am able to laugh at my mistakes.

There is very little about my life I would change.

I feel I am an interesting person.

I like the growth and change I have experienced.

I am kind and loving.

My friends value my opinion.

I am satisfied being who I am.

I am not afraid to express feelings.

I have an interesting and fun life.

3. Close the activity by asking all the students to share one thing they do well and one positive personality characteristic they have.

What's Your Opinion?

Purpose   To encourage critical thought about feelings and beliefs

Materials   None

Procedure   1. Ask students to listen very closely as you read each of the following statements. After giving them a chance to think about the statement, ask them to vote true by thumbs up or false by thumbs down. After each vote, you may wish to call upon individual students to support or explain their thoughts on the matter.

It is good to forget about problems.

You should never feel embarrassed.

Kind people are smart.

Boys are better athletes than girls.

It is all right for adults to act like children.

Everyone becomes bored.

Parents should feel proud.

Funny people are well-liked.

Teachers have a right to lose their cool.

It is good to get excited.

People learn best when they become frustrated.

Being happy is not always desirable.

2. At the close of this activity, ask students what they learned and why it might be important to consider another person's point of view.

Variation   Assign students a particular stand on an issue. Have them debate the topic. The jurors (other students) can vote to determine which stand they feel is most appropriate. (The debates could be videotaped.) Example topics:

Baseball games are boring.

Schools should have dances every weekend.

The legal drinking age should be age 18.

Fears

Purpose　To identify situations that produce fears, stress, or anxiety and to discuss how students can cope with these situations

Materials　Recognizing Fears (Handout 12)

Procedure　1. Start a general discussion by saying that we all have things that we are afraid of. Ask students to share stories about some of the things they were afraid of when they were in grade school (for example, the dark, loud noises, Halloween, big dogs).

2. Pass out the Recognizing Fears worksheet (Handout 12) and ask students to rate themselves on the various items.

3. Ask students to share current situations that they are fearful about or that cause them discomfort. As facilitator, you can also share your own fears.

4. Brainstorm a list of ways people cope with fearful situations. Think of the specific fears discussed and problem-solve solutions. Think about ways parents handle fears of young children.

Variation　Read a book or story containing some frightening element to the group. A good one is *Nightmares: Poems to Trouble Your Sleep,* by Jack Prelutsky (Greenwillow Books, 1976). Have students create some of their own scary poems and fantasies.

RECOGNIZING FEARS

Directions: Rate yourself on the following items by circling the number that best applies to you.

1	2	3	4	5
Very true				Not very true

I worry about schoolwork.

1	2	3	4	5

I get nervous about taking tests.

1	2	3	4	5

I often get headaches or stomachaches.

1	2	3	4	5

I have trouble keeping my mind on one thing.

1	2	3	4	5

I have trouble making decisions.

1	2	3	4	5

I am sometimes afraid to meet new people.

1	2	3	4	5

I feel I am under a great deal of pressure.

1	2	3	4	5

I often don't rest well at night.

1	2	3	4	5

I think that I worry too much.

1	2	3	4	5

Adults expect too much of me.

1	2	3	4	5

I wish I could relax more.

1	2	3	4	5

I am afraid of making mistakes or losing.

1	2	3	4	5

Self-Talk

Purpose   To help students learn about self-talk and how to use affirmations to build self-esteem

Materials   Affirmations for You (Handout 13)

Procedure   1. Tell students that we are always talking to ourselves. These conversations are about past events, current situations, or the future. Much of this talk is negative—we frequently criticize ourselves or put ourselves down. Stress that it is important to become aware of self-talk and try to put ourselves up and be our own best friend.

2. Review the characteristics of self-talk:

   Self-talk is happening all the time.

   We spend more time talking to ourselves than to anyone else.

   Self-talk is usually more negative than positive.

   Self-talk is habit forming and predicts much of our behavior.

   We have control over our self-talk.

   We believe our self-talk, and it affects how we feel about ourselves.

3. Ask students what they have been saying to themselves so far this morning.

4. Ask students to share a message that they give themselves about school, friends, homework, money, or siblings. Reflect that much of this self-talk is negative.

5. Point out that to turn negative self-talk into positive self-talk, we have to be aware of how we are too hard on ourselves, then counter the negative self-talk with positive self-talk. One strategy to enhance self-esteem is to affirm the goodness within us. This can be like self-hypnosis. People can develop a list of affirmations (positive thoughts about themselves) and review them several times a day. An affirmation can also help reinforce personal or academic goals.

6. Pass out the Affirmations for You page (Handout 13) and have students take turns reading each one. Have them circle five they will say to themselves three times a day for the next week. Stress that if they can say the statements for a month, the statements will become true.

Variation   Have small groups of students make posters with one or more of the affirmations on them. Post these around the school.

Handout 13

AFFIRMATIONS FOR YOU

Directions: An affirmation is a positive statement that is true about ourselves or others. It is important to affirm ourselves through positive self-talk. We can also communicate affirmations to others (for example, "You are lovable and capable"). Say these affirmations to yourself and to others.

I am lovable and capable.

I shape my life.

I am a valuable and important person.

I express my feelings as part of myself.

I take pride in my past performances.

I think positive and am optimistic about life.

I have everything I need to enjoy life.

I am honest about myself and trust my feelings.

The more I give, the more I receive.

The more I receive, the more I have to give.

I trust myself in everything I do.

I feel good and share it with others.

It's not what happens to me but how I handle it.

I live every day on purpose, one day at a time.

I grow through all of life's experiences.

I enhance other people's lives.

I bounce back quickly from mistakes or disappointments.

I am a healthy person who grows stronger every day.

Life is for the taking.

I like myself, and that's what counts.

I can relax and let go.

Setting Goals

Purpose   To have students consider what goals they could be setting for themselves

Materials   Chalkboard
Paper and pencils

Procedure   1. Write the following sentence stems on the chalkboard:

Something I want to be better in is . . .

Something new I want to learn is . . .

To take better care of myself I could . . .

To get along better with others I could . . .

At home I want to . . .

2. Have students write their responses down on a sheet of paper.

3. Have them get into groups of three or four and share their responses. Encourage students to write down two things they need to do in order to achieve each of these goals.

4. Collect the responses and keep them so you can pass them back in a month to assess whether students progressed toward any of their goals.

Variation   This can be done as a New Year's resolution activity. Ask students to write three New Year's resolutions. Have them make two copies: one to post in their locker and one as a record for you so you can check how students are doing in a month.

In the Future

Purpose   To help students establish priorities about what is important to them in the future

Materials   Three sets of index cards—each card in a set should have one of the following phrases written on it: *contribution to society, career success, helping others, excitement and adventure, marriage, family, lots of money,* and *creative interests*

Procedure   1. Divide students into three groups and give each group a set of index cards.

2. Have each group arrange the cards in the order that will be most important to them in their adult lives.

3. Have each group share with the other students their arrangement of the cards. Discuss.

Variation   Explain that cable TV, microwaves, personal computers, videocassette recorders, and so on did not exist when you were a child. Ask students to predict what technology and new inventions will be in store for their children.

You Must Have Been a Beautiful Baby

Purpose   To help students become better acquainted with their fellow classmates

Materials   A baby picture of each student
Paper and pencils

Procedure   1. Everyone (including yourself) should bring in a baby picture. If a student cannot find one, then have him or her bring in an early school picture. Make sure the students understand that the purpose of this activity is to see who can correctly identify the most baby pictures. Students should *not* show their pictures to anyone else.

2. Make a display of the photographs, putting a number on or beside each picture. Ask the students to number a sheet of paper and try to guess who is who in the class. After everyone has guessed, identify each student's picture.

3. Ask the students how they have most changed since birth and how their families have changed.

Variations   1. Invite other staff or team members to contribute baby pictures and participate.

2. Ask questions like "How did you get your name?" "What positive childhood experiences can you remember?" and "Who else is in your family?" Discuss heritage.

You're in the News

Purpose   For students to become more aware of their own personal traits

Materials   Old newspapers or magazines
Glue
Scissors
Large index cards

Procedure   1. Give students one index card apiece and have them write their name in the middle of the card. Have students cut words and/or pictures that describe themselves from newspapers or magazines. They should glue these on the index card around their name.

2. Have students explain why they selected the pictures they did for their cards. Staple all cards on the bulletin board for an interesting display.

Variations   1. Use the cards as name tags.

2. Try to find similarities in students' choices:

How many have music represented?

Who has food on his or her card?

Does anyone have a vehicle of some kind?

Whose card shows a sport?

What is the most unusual item chosen?

Signs of Stress

Purpose   To teach students to recognize signs of stress and ways to reduce stress in their lives

Materials   Signs of Stress (Handout 14)

Procedure   NOTE: If a student checks several of the signs of stress, it might be a good idea for that student to talk with the school counselor or social worker.

1. Ask students to brainstorm all the words they can think of when you say the word *stress*.

2. Pass out the Signs of Stress checklist (Handout 14) and have everyone complete it.

3. Have students look over their handouts and discuss which signs are most common and which are least common.

4. Ask students to describe times when they see these signs in themselves, how they feel when they do, and what they can do to reduce the stress.

5. Ask them to suggest ways a close friend or family member who is under a lot of stress might handle it.

Variation   Encourage students to write in a journal or diary about their stress. Sometimes being creative by writing a poem or song is a helpful assignment.

Handout 14

SIGNS OF STRESS

Directions: Put a check mark by the signs of stress you sometimes experience.

☐ Headaches

☐ Stomach problems

☐ High blood pressure or heart pounding

☐ Pain in neck, lower back, shoulders, jaw

☐ Eating problems—no appetite, constantly eating

☐ Sleeping problems—unable to fall asleep, waking up in the middle of the night, nightmares

☐ General feeling of tiredness

☐ Dry throat or mouth

☐ Unable to sit still or extra energy

☐ Stuttering

☐ Crying a lot or not being able to cry

☐ Irritable and easily set off, feeling angry

☐ Feeling overwhelmed or unable to cope, wanting to run away

☐ Feeling that you can't discuss problems with others

☐ Unable to concentrate or finish your work

Stressful Life Events

Purpose To help students learn about events or situations that produce stress or conflict

Materials Chalkboard
Stress Inventory (Handout 15)

Procedure 1. Brainstorm a list of events or situations that produce stress or conflict; write these ideas on the chalkboard. After each example ask the students to identify the feeling associated with the event. Point out that conflict or stress is normal and important for growth and change.

2. Tell students that having to make changes in life causes stress. Give a personal example.

3. Pass out the Stress Inventory (Handout 15) and ask students to check those items that they may have experienced.

4. Ask students to share one of their more stressful life experiences and tell the group how they coped with the situation. See if other students can share ideas of how people cope with similar situations.

5. Discuss how some events can be more stressful than others. Point out that what might be stressful for one person might not be stressful for another.

Variation Have students write a story about what they would consider to be a very stressful day. See whose story has the greatest number of stressful events. You may want to read a related story, such as *Alexander and the Terrible, Horrible, No Good, Very Bad Day,* by Judith Viorst (Macmillan, 1976).

STRESS INVENTORY

Directions: Put a check mark by those life events you have experienced.

☐ Changing to a new school

☐ Family holidays

☐ Death of a pet

☐ Trouble with a teacher

☐ Brother or sister leaves home (for college or military)

☐ Being threatened (by a gang or bully)

☐ Personal achievement or recognition

☐ Moving to a new town

☐ Death or serious illness of a close friend

☐ Parent becomes unemployed (change in financial situation)

☐ Gaining a new family member (birth, adoption, grandparent moving in)

☐ Problems at school

☐ Parents separate or divorce

☐ Death of a close family member

☐ Parents get back together after separation

☐ Remarriage of a parent (getting a new parent)

☐ Major personal injury or illness in family

Other stressful life events *(fill in)*

☐ _____

☐ _____

Heroes

Purpose   To encourage students to think of positive role models, both living people and historical figures

Materials   Chalkboard

Procedure   1. Ask students for their definition of *hero*.

2. Ask everyone in the class to think of a hero that they have or have had as a child. Ask them for one example of a living hero and one example of a nonliving hero. Share responses.

3. Write the following on the chalkboard:

Physical features

Mental features

Social features

Economic features

Personality features

4. Ask students to analyze and define their heroes according to these characteristics and to share their thoughts.

5. Ask students what they have in common with their heroes.

Variations   1. Have students construct their own personal hall of fame by bringing in pictures of their heroes. Encourage them to bring in heroes from different walks of life (science, sports, entertainment, and so forth).

2. Encourage students to write short reports on heroic figures. Have them present the reports to the group or put them in the school newsletter or newspaper. Coordinate reports to special months—for example, Black History Month (February) or Women in History Month (March).

3. Ask students to share about a biography and autobiography they have read.

Talking About Coping

Purpose   To give students an opportunity to share how they cope with the challenges of everyday life

Materials   Chalkboard

Procedure   1. Ask students to think of two things that really bug them. Share an example or two, such as standing in lines, slow drivers, feeling taken for granted or taken advantage of, and so forth. Go around the circle and have students share their examples.

2. Next ask students to think of how they act when they are being bugged. Have each student share his or her responses; write these on the chalkboard.

3. Discuss which responses work best to help students cope with the challenging situations. On the chalkboard, circle the most effective responses. If there are few positive responses, try to brainstorm other strategies. Some examples might include using relaxation skills (deep breathing, visualization, counting), stress management activities (exercising, playing or listening to music, reading or writing, walking), or communication skills (assertiveness, negotiation).

4. Ask students to commit to trying more positive approaches to challenging situations in the future. Ask for examples of situations and coping strategies.

Variation   Go around the circle and have students complete the following sentence stems.

I feel angry when . . .

Something that bugs me about adults is . . .

Something that bugs me at school is . . .

Short Activities About Self

Purpose   To increase students' self-awareness

Materials   None

Procedure   NOTE: Choose from among the following activities as appropriate.

1. Go around the circle and have each person share one thing he or she likes to do and does well.

2. Have each person share three positive words that describe himself or herself.

3. Have students share the last time an adult (teacher or parent) gave them a compliment. What was the compliment?

4. Ask students what record they would break if they could break any record in the world and why.

5. Ask each student to share with the class an area of knowledge or a skill he or she could teach another person. Also ask what each student would like to learn from another person.

6. Ask students to share any accomplishments or recognitions that they have received recently. Give some examples of a wide range of accomplishments—not just finishing first place or getting an A on a test, but reaching other goals as well.

7. Have each student share with the group a favorite memory or joyful experience.

8. Have each student share with the group one trait he or she would like to be remembered for.

Words for Discussion

HAPPINESS

Personalize Who is the happiest person you know?

What makes that person happy?

Some people have trouble having fun—what advice would you give them?

Share an example of a time you were really happy. How did you know you were happy?

Define Happiness = A state of well-being and contentment; the condition of being glad or content.

Challenge What are two things you could do that would help you be happier?

How can you help others around you be happier?

HABIT

Personalize Share one positive habit and one negative habit you have.

What are some of your habits of thought when you think about school? Are these negative or positive habits of thinking? How do they affect your school performance?

Give an example of how a habit is formed.

Define Habit = An action or way of thinking you engage in so often that you do it without thinking—hard to stop and nearly involuntary.

Challenge Share one of your negative habits (behaviors or thoughts) and what you could do to change it.

BOREDOM

Personalize How would your life change if there was no TV?

When do you most often feel bored?

What or who causes boredom?

How can being bored help you?

Define Boredom = A feeling of weariness and dissatisfaction.

Challenge   Share a situation when you felt bored, then something you could have done to keep yourself from being bored.

What can you do when others around you choose to be bored?

How can you be bored less often?

FEAR

Personalize   When you were younger, what was one of your biggest fears?

Do you like to go to scary movies? Why or why not?

Can you share a dream that was frightening?

Define   Fear = An unpleasant, strong emotion caused by anticipation or awareness of danger; concern and worry; apprehensiveness.

Challenge   What is currently one of your biggest fears?

How would your life be different if you didn't have this fear?

What are some ways you might go about overcoming this fear?

EMBARRASSMENT

Personalize   Share a situation at school where you or one of your friends was embarrassed.

What was one of the most embarrassing things that ever happened to you? Are you embarrassed to talk about it?

How do you show your embarrassment (for example, red face, sweating)?

Define   Embarrassment = A feeling of shyness; being ashamed, uncomfortable, or self-conscious.

Challenge   Share a situation that you avoid or are uncomfortable with. Describe your feelings and what you could do to feel more comfortable.

GUILT

Personalize   Share a time when you were a small child and you did something that made you feel guilty.

When you have a guilty conscience about something, do you want to forget about what happened or confess/apologize?

Do you think other people can make you feel guilty, or do you think you choose to make yourself feel that way?

Define   Guilt = A feeling of having done something wrong; shame.

Challenge   If you told your friends everything about yourself, including things you are afraid of or guilty about, do think they would like you more or less than they do now? Why or why not?

LUCK

Personalize   What was the luckiest thing that ever happened to you?

Do you believe in luck, or do people make luck happen?

Is it a waste of money to play the lottery? Why or why not?

Define   Luck = Good fortune; that which happens by chance; "when opportunity meets preparation."

Challenge   Discuss a time when you were hoping for luck instead of being more prepared.

Can you think of any situations where luck might be important to your success?

MOTIVATION

Personalize   Share one thing you are highly motivated to accomplish.

Share one thing you are highly motivated not to do.

What are the strongest motivators for you to get something done (money, threat, fear, sense of pride, fun)?

Define   Motivation = Incentive, drive; the desire to do something.

Challenge   Share something you want to be more motivated to complete. Think of some ways that might help you become motivated to complete the job you have in mind.

HERO

Personalize   When you were younger, who were your heroes?

Who are your heroes today?

Why are these individuals so special?

Define   Hero = A person who is looked up to by others because of his or her great achievements, fine qualities, or image.

Challenge   Think of a person you see every day whom you admire. Discuss the qualities the person has that you also want to develop.

GOAL

Personalize   What would you like to be known for?

What do you want people to say about you at your funeral?

Define   Goal = A direction, end, or place one is striving to reach.

Challenge   Share with the group a goal you have set that relates to achievement in school.

Share a goal you have set for yourself in another part of your life (friends, health, learning, and so forth).

UNIT FOUR

Communication and Conflict Resolution

If we are to reach real peace in this world, we shall have to begin teaching the children.

Gandhi

Overview

This unit includes activities designed to help students improve their communication skills and resolve conflicts. It makes use of the decision-making and brainstorming processes described at some length in the Introduction.

Communication is a basic skill for building relationships and social competencies. Both a sender and receiver phenomenon, it involves listening, summarizing, and clarifying messages, as well as building on new information and feelings. When communication breaks down, conflict often is the result. Conflicts are a part of everyday life. Because of the competitive nature of our society, conflicts are often seen as contests to be won or lost. Unresolved conflicts often result in hurt feelings, lost friendships, increased anger or frustration, and sometimes physical violence.

We often ignore or avoid conflicts because we lack the knowledge and skills to resolve them. However, conflicts can be seen as positive forces that accompany change and growth. Knowing how to handle conflict promotes peace and fairness through a developed sensitivity that is respectful of individual differences.

Conflict generally arises from limited resources, differing values, and/or unmet needs. When conflict arises, most people react with verbal or physical aggression, ignore it, or withdraw and blame themselves. Helping students identify the source of conflict and how they react to it is the first step in resolving problems.

Knowing what we want and need is also basic to resolving a conflict. We have in common the basic needs of belonging, power, freedom, and fun. Conflict resolution is based on looking at what we have in common and making a commitment to cooperate in order to create new possibilities that meet our needs and are beneficial to all involved.

The tools needed for conflict resolution are good communication and decision-making skills. Communication skills are based on active listening and asserting wants or needs. Problem solving involves brainstorming options and choosing a solution that meets needs through compromise. These skills will empower students to solve their own problems and learn from challenging situations.

Activities

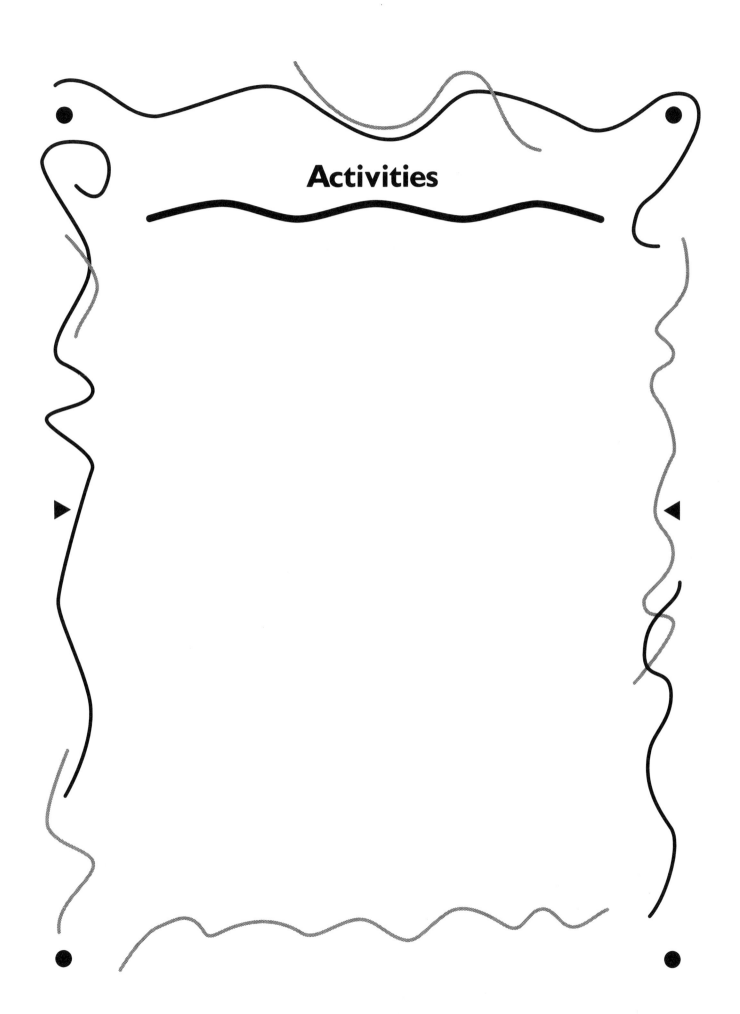

Focus on Listening

Purpose   To teach listening skills and make students aware of the challenges
of effective communication

Materials   Paper and pencils
Listening Diagram 1 (Handout 16)
Listening Diagram 2 (Handout 17)

Procedure   1. Ask one student to be the group leader. Give that student a copy
of Listening Diagram 1 (Handout 16) without letting anyone else
in the class view it. Explain to the class that they will draw on a
piece of paper the diagram the group leader will describe to them.
Explain the following rules:

Instructions will be given and then repeated only once.

No one may ask any questions.

Rulers and other measuring instruments may not be used.

2. Ask the group leader to stand in front of the class and call out one
line or shape at a time in a clear, loud voice. The leader should
repeat these instructions once before going on to the next line or
shape. For example: "Draw a square 2 inches on all sides in the
middle of your paper. *(Repeat instruction.)* Next, inside the square,
draw a circle almost as large as the square. *(Repeat instruction.)*"

3. After students have completed their drawings, ask the following
questions:

Was this exercise difficult for you?

Why did people draw different diagrams from the same
instructions?

What are some of the problems that got in the way of good
communication?

How is this exercise different from other kinds of communication?
How is it similar?

4. Repeat the activity with a new group leader and Listening
Diagram 2 (Handout 17), but this time let the group ask questions.

5. Discuss the differences between the nonquestion and question
situations.

Handout 16

LISTENING DIAGRAM 1

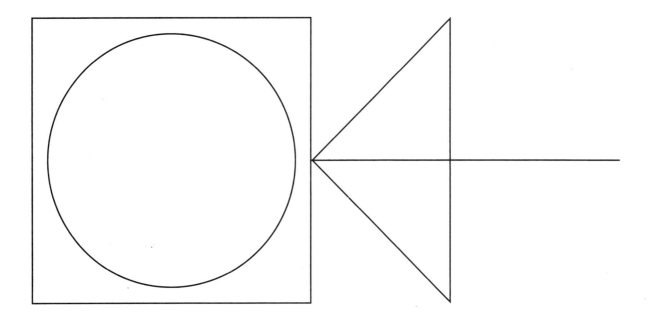

Handout 17

LISTENING DIAGRAM 2

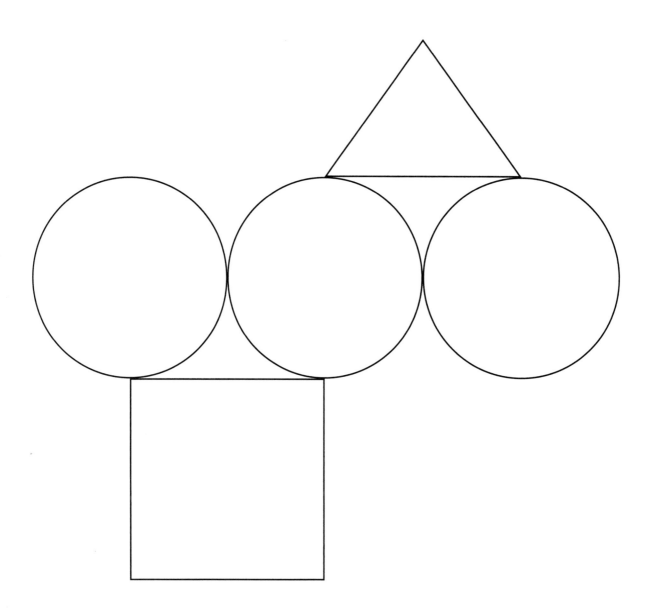

ACTIVITY 48

Show You're Listening

Purpose To improve listening skills

Materials Chalkboard

Procedure 1. Ask the question "How do you show someone you are listening?" Make a list of responses on the chalkboard. Elicit the following responses:

Eye contact

Posture (leaning forward)

Facial expression

Nodding

Not interrupting

2. Divide the class into pairs. Have one person be the speaker and one person be the listener. Start by having one student talk for a minute and the other student practice being a good listener. Afterwards, ask the speaker, "How did it feel to be listened to uninterrupted?" Ask the listener, "How did it feel to listen and not ask questions?"

3. Have the pairs switch roles. Ask the speaker and listener the same questions you did before.

4. Have students choose a new partner to practice summarizing what they hear. The listener must restate the highlights of what is being said. This checks for understanding facts and feelings. Before beginning, demonstrate this to the class by asking one student to briefly tell the group about an after-school plan. You should then summarize in a brief statement.

5. Let students practice listening and summarizing in pairs. Let the speaker talk for only 30 seconds, then ask the listener to summarize. The person who talks can choose any topic (school, vacation, sports, family, and so on). Give everyone a chance at each role.

6. Ask students to have a 3-minute conversation with someone in which they summarize the other person's statement before they make one of their own. Demonstrate this process with a student before having the other students practice.

Dealing With Put-Downs

Purpose   To help students become more aware of the various types of put-downs and how to handle them in a positive way

Materials   Chalkboard

Procedure   1. Define put-downs as things we do or say that are negative messages about ourselves or other people. Describe three kinds of put-downs and give examples of each:

Others can put you down—for example, "You got a D on that test? Are you that dumb, or were you just asleep?"

You can put other people down—for example, "It makes me laugh every time I see how stupid you look when you try to dance."

You can put yourself down—for example, "There isn't much reason why anyone would really want to be my friend."

2. Ask the question "What can you do or say when another student puts you down?" Brainstorm and list on the chalkboard a number of possible responses:

Ignore it or walk away.

Cut the person off with a quick comeback—for example, "I don't agree," "Big deal," "Really? I didn't know that."

Agree with the person—for example, "Yeah, you're right," "Who told you?"

Make a joke of it—for example, "Are you sure you're talking to the right person?" "Would you put that in writing?" "I just love your sense of humor."

3. Brainstorm a list of possible responses when an adult puts you down. For example:

That doesn't help me very much.

I feel bad when you say things like that.

That's not a helpful comment.

4. Brainstorm things you can say to yourself about a person who puts you down. For example:

Kids who put others down usually feel bad about themselves.

Something else must be bugging that kid.

He's trying to impress those other people.

She's trying to act cool. She must not like herself.

I wonder what's wrong with him today?

5. Elicit examples of put-downs students have experienced or seen. Role-play responses to these situations as students generate them.

Being Assertive: How to Say No and Mean It

Purpose To encourage students to express their preferences assertively

Materials Chalkboard

Procedure
1. Ask students to give examples of situations in which they felt pressured to do something that they did not want to do. List at least five examples on the chalkboard.

2. Explain the following strategies for refusing something without losing friends or making people angry.

   Take your stand—Refuse politely and explain your reason. Repeat it in a variety of ways.

   Avoid excuses—Stick to the original reason you gave; be a "broken record."

   Tell the person how you feel when you are pressured—Turn the pressure back on that person.

   Change the subject—Refuse to discuss it because you won't change your mind; change the subject to something more positive.

   Compromise—Work out an arrangement that is as satisfying as possible for both of you.

3. Using the example situations the students gave, take each of the five strategies and role-play one situation to a successful ending.

4. Use other student examples to role-play ways to combine several of the five strategies.

The Accident Report

Purpose To show the importance of listening and to illustrate how people's memories and perceptions can change events

Materials None

Procedure
1. Explain to students that the group will be doing a communication exercise. Select three students to leave the room.

2. Read "The Accident Report" aloud one time to the rest of the group.

   The Accident Report

   I saw this incredible accident! A motorcycle, BMW, Ford pick-up, and Volvo station wagon all pull up to this four-way stop at the same time. Nobody knows what to do. They all sit for a while, then start waving each other to go. Then they all go at the same time. The Volvo plows into the pick-up and knocks these crates of pigs out of the back. The crates burst open, and all of a sudden there are a dozen pigs running around. The BMW and motorcycle manage to avoid hitting the other cars, but the BMW hits a fire hydrant and water starts shooting 50 feet into the air, soaking everything.

3. Next bring one of the students who left the room back into the group. Call upon one student (Student A) from the group who heard you read the accident report to repeat the story as accurately as possible to the student who just came in (Student B).

4. Next bring in another student who had been outside the room (Student C) and have Student B repeat the report as accurately as possible to Student C.

5. Have the remaining student who was outside the room (Student D) come back into the group. Have Student C repeat the report as accurately as possible to Student D.

6. Ask Student D to repeat the report to the entire group. Discuss how the report changed and how what students have learned in this activity might apply to real-life situations.

Clear Communications

Purpose To teach the importance of clear communications

Materials Blindfold
Bread
Peanut butter
Jelly
Knife
Plate

Procedure 1. Select two students from the group and blindfold one of them. Place a knife, plate, and sandwich materials on a table or desk. Have the blindfolded student wait at the door. Tell this student that he or she can say nothing.

2. Ask the other student to give directions to walk over to the table, make a peanut butter and jelly sandwich, and bring it to you.

3. After you receive the sandwich, ask the students the following questions:

How well were directions followed?

What was said that helped the job get done?

What was said that confused the sandwich maker?

4. Repeat the exercise several times with other students.

Variations 1. During one exercise let the sandwich maker ask questions to see how that changes the process.

2. Change the activity to involve directions for other tasks—for example, folding a paper airplane, finding an object placed in the room, or finding two group members and having them shake hands.

Steps in Decision Making

Purpose To make students more aware of the number of decisions that they make every day and present the five steps in the decision-making process

Materials Chalkboard

Procedure NOTE: See the Introduction for more information about the decision-making process used in this activity.

1. Have students brainstorm a list of decisions that they have made already today. For example:

   What to wear

   What to eat for breakfast

   How to get to school

   Whom to talk to before school

   Whether to come to school or not

2. Point out that we are always making decisions about what we choose to do. Some of these decisions help us reach our goals, and some slow us down or stop us from achieving.

3. Ask students the following questions:

   How do you decide whom to sit with at lunch?

   How do you decide whether to do your homework or not?

   How do you decide when to go to bed on weekends?

   How do you decide what activities to do with your friends?

4. Explain to students that in making any decision, there are some steps to follow. Write these steps on the chalkboard.

   Step 1: Define the problem

   Step 2: Think of possible options

   Step 3: Review your options and choose one

   Step 4: Act on your choice

   Step 5: Evaluate your actions

5. Select one of the following situations and go through the five steps to make a group decision.

You and a friend are trying to decide what to do on a Saturday afternoon.

You need to raise 20 dollars to go on a trip to an amusement park (and your parents won't give you the money).

You are invited to go to a party (which you really want to go to) but have already made a commitment to baby-sit (and you really need the money).

Brainstorming

Purpose   To teach students how to brainstorm and to suggest that they have more choices to solve problems than they might imagine

Materials   Paper and pencils

Procedure   NOTE: See the Introduction for more information about the brainstorming process used in this activity.

1. Explain the rules for brainstorming:

   Say any ideas that come to mind.

   Don't judge or discuss the ideas.

   Build on all the ideas given.

   Be spontaneous and creative.

   Come up with as many ideas as possible.

2. Have students divide into groups of three to five each and brainstorm a list of possible uses for a brick. Give them 5 minutes to come up with at least 20 ideas or more.

3. Have groups share their entire lists with the class.

4. Ask each group to go back through their list and circle the three uses they think are the most creative solutions, then share these responses with the class.

5. Discuss how creative the lists are and how many options we often have that we don't at first realize.

Variation   Ask students to brainstorm all the uses for a paper clip, a ball of yarn, a bag of marshmallows, a hula hoop, and so forth.

Conflict in the News

Purpose To help students realize how common conflicts are in the world today

Materials Newspapers and magazines
Poster board
Scissors
Glue

Procedure 1. Explain to students that this is a world in which not everyone agrees. Because there are differences, there are conflicts. Give a few examples of conflicts in current news stories.

2. Have students look through newspapers and magazines and cut out an article or picture that shows a conflict.

3. Have students report on the event, then glue the article or picture to the poster board. You will accumulate a collage of conflicts.

Variations 1. Have each student select one of the articles. His or her job is to write a follow-up story creating a peaceful ending.

2. Collect the covers of *Time* or *Newsweek* magazines. Have students discuss the issues and conflicts happening each week.

3. Discuss what the group could do to make the world more peaceful if they were in charge.

ACTIVITY 56

Understanding Conflict

Purpose   To help students identify the types of conflicts they have with peers, siblings, and teachers, as well as conflicts in the news

To discuss the origins of these conflicts and help students evaluate how they react

Materials   Chalkboard
Conflict and You (Handout 18)

Procedure   NOTE: This activity has been adapted from *Peer Mediation: Conflict Resolution in Schools*, by Fred Schrumpf, Donna Crawford, and H. Chu Usadel, 1991, Champaign, IL: Research Press.

1. Write the word *conflict* on the chalkboard. Have students come up with words they associate with conflict (for example, *fight, argument, war, disagreement, hassle*).

2. Divide the class into groups of three to five students each. Assign each group the task of writing a list of conflicts. Give each group a specific category: conflicts with peers, siblings, or teachers, or conflicts in the news (local, national, worldwide).

3. After 10 minutes, have each group share their list. Point out that conflicts are a part of everyday life. Tell students that we can learn from conflicts. They test our abilities and skills in communication and problem solving.

4. Refer students to the Conflict and You form (Handout 18). Ask them to think of a recent conflict, then fill out Part I of the handout to describe it. Give them 5 minutes to do this, then have several students share their responses with the class.

5. Next ask students to fill out Part II of the handout. After they have finished, read this checklist aloud and have students raise their hands if the response is true for them. Point out that different people respond differently depending on the situation.

127

Handout 18

CONFLICT AND YOU

Part I

Directions: Answer the following questions.

Describe a personal conflict and the person it involved. _____

_____

What were some of the feelings you had about the conflict? _____

_____

How did you act in the situation? _____

_____

How did the other person act? _____

_____

What did you want in order for the conflict to be over? _____

_____

Part II

Directions: When you are angry, hurt, or upset, how do you handle conflict? Check the three you do most often.

☐ Avoid or ignore the situation.

☐ Threaten the other person.

☐ Fight it out physically.

☐ Just give in because it doesn't really matter.

☐ Try to reach a compromise.

☐ Complain until you get your way.

☐ Get another person to decide who is right.

☐ Admit you were wrong, even if you don't think so.

☐ Change the subject.

☐ Try to understand the other person's point of view.

ACTIVITY 56

Contest or Conflict?

Purpose   To demonstrate that we often see a situation as a contest with
a winner and a loser when we could look at the situation in
a more cooperative way

Materials   Table and chairs
A prize (for example, pencil or candy bar)

Procedure   1. Set up three or four pairs of students in arm-wrestling positions
at a table.

2. Explain the mission: "Your challenge is to get the person's hand
across from you down as many times as you can in 30 seconds.
Each time a hand touches the table, return to the starting position
as quickly as possible and start again. A prize will be awarded to
the two individuals who have the most points."

3. Have someone keep the time. Tell pairs to begin.

4. Observe the contest. Most pairs will struggle to win a point;
however, some may offer no resistance and alternately put
each other's hand down quickly many times.

5. When the time is up, award the prize and process the activity by
discussing the difference between the competitive (win/lose) and
the cooperative (win/win) way of looking at the challenge. Ask the
following questions:

Why did some pairs compete and others cooperate?

What real-life situations are often viewed as contests, with
a winner and loser, when cooperation may work better?

What happens in a competitive situation when one person
is so much stronger that the other person gives up?

What are the long-term consequences of domination?

Brainstorming Solutions to Conflict Situations

Purpose To teach students how to create many options when trying to solve a problem

Materials Chalkboard

Procedure NOTE: See the Introduction for more information about the brainstorming process used in this activity.

1. Point out that in order to resolve conflicts, it is necessary to realize that there are many possible solutions to a problem. Because we get upset or frustrated, we often do not consider all of our options. Brainstorming is a technique that is used to help people come up with as many ideas as possible to solve a problem.

2. Review the rules for brainstorming:

   Say any ideas that come to mind.

   Don't judge or discuss the ideas.

   Build on all the ideas given.

   Be spontaneous and creative.

   Come up with as many ideas as possible.

3. Select a situation from the following list and encourage students to brainstorm all of the possible solutions. Write the ideas on the chalkboard.

   Someone keeps teasing you and calling you names on the bus.

   You lend another student your Walkman, and the teacher confiscates it.

   Your teacher accuses you of cheating on a test.

   Someone says he or she saw your girlfriend or boyfriend holding hands with someone else at the mall yesterday.

   Your parents ground you for a week for fighting with your younger brother.

   The person behind you keeps hitting you in the head with rubber bands during class.

   You didn't get invited to a party to which your friends were invited.

4. After students have generated a list of options, discuss which options might work best. Circle the two best choices.

5. Repeat with as many other situations as time permits. Students may also role-play these conflicts, ending with positive outcomes.

Negotiation

Purpose To help students learn to negotiate and compromise when making requests

Materials Chalkboard

Procedure 1. Explain that requests made of others are often denied. Rather than getting angry or walking away, people can reach an agreement through a compromise arrived at through *negotiation*.

2. Encourage students to give examples of situations in which they have made a request that was denied. (Often such requests are made of parents or teachers.)

3. Tell students that, when negotiating, they need to do as follows:

Find a good time to talk.

Never negotiate with an angry person.

Stay calm yourself.

Leave if told to—ask to talk later.

4. Write on the chalkboard and discuss the specific steps to follow when negotiating:

Step 1: Make your request.

Step 2: When you see there is a difference of opinion, ask the other person how he or she thinks the difference can be worked out.

Step 3: Show you are listening by summarizing the response and telling the other person what you think about the problem.

Step 4: Propose a compromise.

5. Role-play students' example situations. Have students use the steps and work out a solution that meets everyone's needs.

The Mediation Process

Purpose To teach students the steps in the mediation process and to encourage their use

Materials Mediation Process Summary (Handout 19)

Procedure NOTE: This activity has been adapted from *Peer Mediation: Conflict Resolution in Schools,* by Fred Schrumpf, Donna Crawford, and H. Chu Usadel, 1991, Champaign, IL: Research Press.

1. Introduce the idea that successful conflict resolution is a win/win strategy in which both parties are willing to respect each other, listen to different points of view, and compromise. Tell students that in order to resolve conflict, people must be willing to do as follows:

    Stay calm and control their anger

    Focus on the problem and not the person (no name-calling, blaming, or interrupting)

    Honestly state their feelings and needs

    Listen to the other person's point of view

    Brainstorm and choose a solution that meets the needs of everyone involved

2. Define *mediation* as a skill used for resolving conflicts in which a third person acts as a neutral outside party to help disputants negotiate. Point out that mediation can be very successful when two peers have a conflict and state the ground rules for mediation:

    The mediator does not take sides.

    Each person explains his or her side of the story, uninterrupted.

    Mediations are held confidential.

    Both people agree to work together toward a resolution.

3. Distribute the Mediation Process Summary (Handout 19). Discuss the six steps in the mediation process.

4. After reviewing the steps, ask two students to volunteer to participate in a role-play as disputants. (You should play the part of the mediator.) Choose one of the following situations for the role-play.

A student keeps butting in front of you in the lunch line.

You loaned a library book to a classmate. It is overdue at the library, but the classmate says it was returned.

Someone on the bus keeps calling you and your mother names.

One of your best friends is invited to a party to which you have not been invited. You respond by ignoring that friend.

5. Discuss the role-play. Ask the disputants how they felt about the process. Ask the group if they thought the agreement reached was realistic and balanced. Were there any suggestions for the mediator? What situations have they experienced in which a mediator would have been helpful?

6. Conduct another role-play, this time with a student as mediator. Practice additional mediations as time allows.

7. Ask students if they can give examples of situations where mediation might work for disputes between friends, family members, or neighbors. Ask them whether students have ever informally mediated between two disputing parties.

MEDIATION PROCESS SUMMARY

Step 1: Open the session

Make introductions.

State the ground rules.

Get a commitment to follow the ground rules.

Step 2: Gather information

Ask each person (one at a time) for his or her side of the story.

Listen, summarize, clarify.

Repeat the process by asking for additional information.

Listen, summarize, clarify.

Step 3: Focus on common interests

Determine what each person wants and why the person wants it.

State the common interests.

Step 4: Create options

Explain that a brainstorming process will be used to find solutions that satisfy both persons.

State the rules for brainstorming.

Help the brainstorming process along by asking questions.

Step 5: Evaluate options and choose a solution

Evaluate the list of options.

Decide on one that best meets the needs of both persons.

Summarize the agreement.

Step 6: Write the agreement down and shake hands

Tough Decisions Box

Purpose   To practice a decision-making model and give students an opportunity to address student concerns

Materials   A shoe box

Procedure   1. Introduce the activity by bringing in a "Dear Abby" column from the newspaper. Read the column. Explain that people write in about a problem and are looking for advice.

2. Explain that students will have an opportunity to write in questions, concerns, or personal problems to the Tough Decisions Box and to get advice from the group. Discuss the types of questions students might submit. For example:

I'm new at school and want to make friends, but no one seems very friendly to me.

I don't get along with one of my teachers and have already received two detentions.

I loaned a friend 2 dollars 2 weeks ago, and the person won't pay me back. I need the cash now.

Two different boys asked me to the school dance, and I can't decide which one to go with.

3. Each week (or bimonthly), select one of the questions and work through the decision-making process detailed in the Introduction of this book in order to identify the best choice. Briefly, the steps in this process are as follows:

Step 1: Define the problem

Step 2: Think of possible options

Step 3: Review your options and choose one

Step 4: Act on your choice

Step 5: Evaluate your actions

4. Tell students that the questions should not be signed so they can feel free to write about any concern.

Decisions, Decisions, Decisions

Purpose   To help students identify the variety and quality of decisions they make

Materials   Chalkboard
Paper and pencils

Procedure   1. Write the following on the chalkboard:

A time I made a good decision

A time I made a bad decision

A time when I couldn't make a decision

A decision I made that my parents were proud of

A decision I made to please my friends

A decision I made that didn't please my friends

2. Have students choose three of these items to respond to in writing.

3. Go through the list and ask for volunteers to read their responses. Share some of your responses as well.

4. Ask students what the main factors are that they consider before making a decision. Do they usually make decisions quickly or think about them for a long time?

5. Finally, ask students to share a current decision they have been thinking about. Use the problem-solving steps listed in Activity 61 and see if a good decision is reached.

Conflict in Children's Books

Purpose   To discuss the sources of conflict as shown in children's literature

Materials   A children's book or books of your choice

Procedure   Many children's books deal with the common theme of conflict. Some of these conflicts occur because of differing perceptions or values. Discuss the relevance of the stories you read to students' current issues or concerns. Some good ones to try are as follows.

The Mystery Beast of Ostergeest, by Steven Kellogg (Dial, 1971). A short story about six wise blind men and an elephant. Each perceives the same elephant to be something totally different.

The Island of the Skog, by Steven Kellogg (Dial, 1976). A short book that tells a story about how assumptions and perceptions affect our behaviors.

Roots in the Outfield, by Jane Zirpoli (Houghton Mifflin, 1988). A 150-page book dealing with name-calling, the challenges of new family relationships, the joys of new friendships, and conquering fears.

Fables, by Arnold Lobel (Harper and Row, 1980). A collection of 21 contemporary fables with unexpected morals. The "Bad Kangaroo" is an especially good one for student behaviors.

The True Story of the Three Little Pigs, by J. Scieszka (Viking, 1989). A very short story telling this traditional tale from the wolf's perspective and showing that there are two sides to any story.

The Lorax, by Dr. Seuss (Random House, 1971). A story with implications about the environment and the long-term consequences of business decisions.

The Sneetches and Other Stories, by Dr. Seuss (Random House, 1961). Four short stories featuring the Sneetches, characters who deal with issues of prejudice and discrimination.

The Butter Battle Book, by Dr. Seuss (Random House, 1984). A short story about how conflicts can escalate with no winners.

Choosing to Become Angry

Purpose   To show students that we all handle anger differently and that we can choose the way we express anger

Materials   Handling Anger Worksheet (Handout 20)

Procedure   1. Ask each student to describe the last time he or she was angry. Ask students to share with whom they were angry, why they were angry, and how they showed their anger.

2. Pass out the Handling Anger Worksheet (Handout 20). Have students get into groups of three or four, fill out Part I of the worksheet, and share responses.

3. Reassemble the larger group. Use examples from the handout and brainstorm some alternative ways of handling anger. For example:

   Tell another person that you are angry and why.

   Use humor to ease the situation.

   Work out a compromise.

   Walk away.

   Count to 10 backwards.

   Take three deep breaths.

4. Next discuss the following questions:

   Why do we choose to be angry rather than choosing to be calm?

   Does getting angry help you get what you want?

   Why do some people choose to get more angry than others?

5. Have students write their responses to the situations found in Part II of the handout. Discuss as a group.

Handout 20

HANDLING ANGER WORKSHEET

Part I

Directions: List the last three times you were angry. Include (a) with whom you were angry, (b) why you were angry, and (c) how you showed your anger.

1. (a) _____

   (b) _____

   (c) _____

2. (a) _____

   (b) _____

   (c) _____

3. (a) _____

   (b) _____

   (c) _____

Part II

Directions: Tell what you would do in the following situations.

1. You and another person want to use the same video game at the same time.

2. Someone pushes you in front of your friends.

3. A teacher makes you do something that you don't want to do.

4. Someone insults your mother in front of friends.

5. Your parents ground you for the weekend due to poor grades.

Short Activities About Conflict

Purpose To increase students' awareness and understanding of conflict

Materials As specified in each activity

Procedure NOTE: Choose from among the following activities as appropriate.

1. Read a book aloud in which conflict is a major theme. Identify the conflict and how the characters dealt with the effects and consequences.

2. Have students think of a conflict in a film they have seen. How was the conflict handled? What happened? Make connections between their examples and real-life situations they may encounter.

3. Draw a diagram of an escalator (or steps) on the chalkboard. Pick a conflict situation a student has and on each step write what happens as the conflict escalates. Discuss what would need to happen for this conflict to deescalate.

4. As a group, pick a conflict that exists in your school (such as two groups that don't get along) or in the community (such as two neighbors who don't get along). Make a plan to improve the situation.

5. Pick a subject of conflict (for example, a child who refuses to clean his or her room or to do homework). Write the position taken by each disputant (parent-child or teacher-child). Focus on each disputant one at a time and try to understand each one's perspective. List on the chalkboard the position and feelings both sides may have. Discuss common interests and possible solutions.

6. Discuss what would be needed for there to be peace in the world. If we had peace, what would it look like? Do we need war to make peace? Encourage students to interview older people about what peace means to them.

7. Create a short story with a conflict but no ending. Divide into four groups and have each group develop a different ending to the story: win-lose, win-win, lose-win, and lose-lose.

8. Create some short skits about conflicts and present them to younger students to teach them healthier ways to deal with conflict.

9. Have the group play a short board game or card game, then process what happened. Who won? Did conflict occur? How was it handled?

Words for Discussion

RUMOR

Personalize When has a rumor hurt your feelings?

Why do people start rumors and gossip?

What do you think of the rumor that girls start more rumors than boys?

Why do rumors hurt a person's reputation rather than help it?

Define Rumor = A story or report circulating without known foundation or authority; common gossip; hearsay.

Challenge What are responsible choices for you to make when you hear a rumor? Next time you hear a rumor, make a responsible choice.

APPROVAL

Personalize We seek approval from many different sources in our life (parents, teachers, friends, coaches, and so on). Which source is most important to you?

Do you act differently around friends, teachers, parents? Is it possible to get approval from all groups?

How do you express approval or disapproval of others?

Define Approval = Favorable opinion, praise; the view of a person as worthy, proper, or right.

Challenge Give an example of something you would do that would gain approval from one group but disapproval from another. How would you make a decision about what to do?

ANGER

Personalize Give an example of a time you were angry during the last week. How did you act?

What happens when you choose to lose your temper?

What are ways that you have found to help keep your anger in control?

Define Anger = A strong or violent displeasure; a result of opposition; rage.

Challenge   Think of someone with whom you got angry. Practice giving feedback to that person in a constructive way. Next time you get angry, what are you going to try?

PUT-DOWN

Personalize   Brainstorm a list of the most frequently heard put-downs at school.

What are some of the reasons that people put others down?

How do you react when someone puts you down?

Define   Put-down = A comment that humbles or deflates, as a cutting remark; making fun or teasing someone.

Challenge   Try to go through a day and not put other people down.

Try to go through a day without putting yourself down.

Decide that you will not let anyone put you down. How will you act if someone does?

THREAT

Personalize   Think of a time you were threatened. What was the situation and how did it feel?

When you feel threatened, do you want to fight, come back with a threat, or walk away?

Why do some people constantly threaten other people?

Define   Threat = A declaration of an intention to inflict pain or injury; any menace or danger.

Challenge   What is your best strategy if you have been threatened and you don't want the threat to become a reality?

If you see someone else being threatened, how could you help?

HATE

Personalize   Finish this sentence: "I hate _____."

Is hate too strong a word for a personal dislike?

What might be a better word than hate?

Define   Hate = Very strong feelings against; strong dislike; intense hostility and aversion, usually deriving from anger or fear.

Challenge   Discuss one thing that you hate and why you hate it. Ask yourself if it is helpful to hate something so strongly.

Why is there so much hatred in the world?

SELF-CONTROL

Personalize   Share a time when you think you lost control—when you said, "I can't help it."

What emotions did the situation stimulate (anger, fear, excitement, frustration)?

Why did you choose to lose control? If you can't help it, who can? Don't some people choose to stay in control?

Define   Self-control = A choice we make that determines our behaviors and attitudes; self-discipline, restraint.

Challenge   What are you going to tell yourself the next time you feel as though you are losing control?

CONFLICT

Personalize   What conflicts have you recently seen in the news?

What are the sources of many of these conflicts?

Describe a conflict that you have been having with yourself.

Define   Conflict = A difference or disagreement; state of opposition or contradictory impulses, ideas, or beliefs.

Challenge   Think of a conflict in the world. What might happen if there is no resolution? What could be done to work it out?

Think of a personal conflict. What steps do you need to take in order to bring about resolution?

DISCRIMINATION

Personalize   Share a time you felt you were discriminated against because of your age.

When have you seen someone being discriminated against because of race?

Think of ways that you are part of the majority group (the insiders). Think of ways you are part of the minority group (the outsiders).

Define   Discrimination = Action taken with partiality; biased or unfair treatment or judgment.

Challenge   Think of ways you might sometimes discriminate against people of a different race, sex, or age.

APPEARANCE

Personalize On a scale of 1 to 10, how important is your appearance?

Would you shave your head for 100 dollars and then go to school?

Share an example of a time you made fun of someone else because of the clothes the person wore or the person's general appearance.

If the school had uniforms, what would you choose for everyone to wear?

Define Appearance = One's external aspects; what is visible.

Challenge Come to school dressed differently than you usually do.
Dress up and/or dress down and see the reactions.

UNIT FIVE

Relating to Others

If we cannot reconcile all opinions, let us endeavor to unite all hearts.

Robert Owen

Overview

Probably the most significant developmental issue for young adolescents is peer relationships. At this age, friendships are extremely important. These friendships are often fragile and changing. Same-sex friendships continue to be very important, but new interests and attractions toward the opposite sex gain in importance. Your students have a great interest and need to think and talk about peer relationships. Making decisions as an individual within the dynamics of a peer group is one of the challenges of this age; the feelings associated with wanting to fit in yet maintain one's individuality are confusing. The activities in this unit concern relationships with others—peers, family, and others in the school and larger community.

In addition, schools today represent a diverse population with various cultures, ethnic groups, and backgrounds. A certain level of understanding and sensitivity is needed for students to work, play, and learn together. A basic understanding of how people differ includes awareness and acceptance of differences in race, gender, ethnic background, age, disability, and religion. A number of the activities in this unit focus on such issues.

Activities

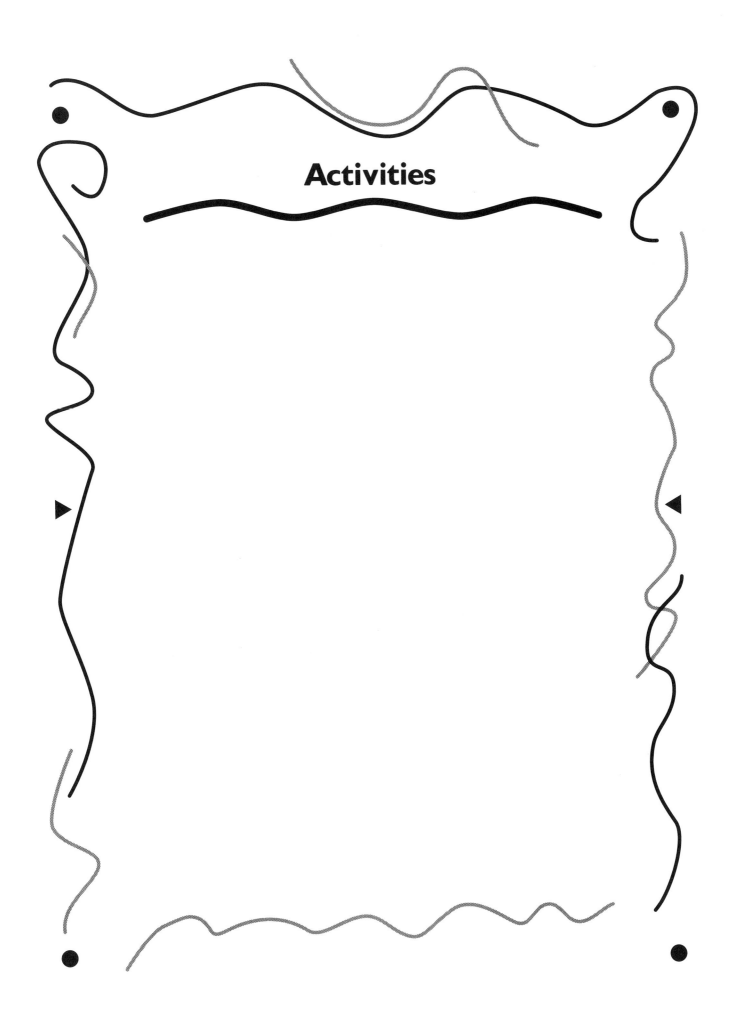

Fishbowl of Feelings

Purpose To give students a forum for discussing questions and feelings about relationships

Materials A small fishbowl (a jar will do)
Slips of paper and pencils

Procedure 1. Explain to students that there are always a lot of questions and feelings when it comes to relationships with peers. Point out that relationships have pressures and patterns that are challenging for everyone.

2. Have students write at least one question they might have about their relationships or themselves and place it in the bowl. Leave the bowl on your desk so students can write questions during the week.

3. Once a week, select two or three questions to share with the group for discussion and problem solving. Be sure to select questions that will generate discussion and can generalize to other students. Use the brainstorming and decision-making processes described in the Introduction to explore possibilities.

4. Leave the bowl out for a month to see what types of questions are submitted. This is an activity that you can do for the entire year.

Variations 1. Use the fishbowl of feelings as the basis for an advice column in the school newsletter or newspaper.

2. Invite parents to submit questions—have the students respond in the school newsletter.

Looking at Relationships

Purpose   To give students an opportunity to share their thoughts and feelings about relationships

Materials   None

Procedure

1. Go around the circle and have each student complete the following sentence stems:

   One of my favorite people is . . .

   I like it when my mother/father . . .

   What I like about my friends is . . .

   I don't like it when my friends . . .

   My family likes to . . .

2. Encourage students to share their responses to the following situations. Be sure to share your own responses as well.

   If your best friend was willing to be honest and tell you exactly what he or she likes most about you, what do you think the person would say?

   If your best friend was willing to be honest and tell you exactly what he or she likes least about you, what do you think the person would say?

   What do you think is the most important thing about being a friend?

   What do you think is the most important thing about being a parent?

Qualities in a Friend

Purpose To clarify qualities most important in friendships

Materials Chalkboard
Slips of paper and pencils

Procedure 1. Ask students to brainstorm a list of qualities it takes to be a good friend. List at least 10 responses on the chalkboard. For example:

Kind to others

Loyal

Athletic

Intelligent

Good sense of humor

Talkative

Popular

Attractive

Honest

Outgoing

Gets good grades

Has money

2. Divide into groups of three to four students. Have the groups write the qualities on separate slips of paper, then rank the qualities from most to least important. Have groups share their responses.

3. Discuss the following questions:

Is the ranking your group chose true for you individually?

How do friendships change at different times and in different situations?

Are there other qualities of friendships not listed?

What is the most important quality in a friend?

Is it important to have a "best friend"?

Variation Ask students to think of a friendship they currently have. Have them suggest one way in which they might improve the friendship and one way in which their friend might improve the relationship. List these ideas in two columns on the chalkboard. Compare and contrast the lists.

Girlfriends and Boyfriends

Purpose   To encourage students to clarify what traits are important to them in a girlfriend or boyfriend

Materials   Paper and pencils

Procedure
1. Divide into two groups, boys on one side and girls on the other. You may want to break each group again to form even smaller groups.

2. Ask the girls to make a list of the 10 qualities that they think the ideal boyfriend should have. Ask the boys to develop a list of the 10 qualities of the ideal girlfriend.

3. When finished, ask both groups to circle the three most important qualities for boyfriends and for girlfriends. Have each group read their list and indicate what the top three qualities are.

4. Discuss the following questions:

   How are these qualities different for boys and girls?

   Are top qualities based on looks or personality?

   How important is the person's appearance?

   How important is the person's intelligence?

   Do you think your parents would have a similar ranking?

   What other qualities could be added to the list?

ACTIVITY 70

Making Friends

Purpose To encourage students to reflect on making and building friendships

Materials Chalkboard
Paper and pencils

Procedure
1. Explain to the group that most every student will gain or lose friends throughout life. This is a great experience, but it is sometimes painful. Friendships are ever changing, just as we grow and change. One thing is sure: No one can have too many friends.

2. Tell students that you are going to write a group poem called "Friendship." Write the following sentence stem on the chalkboard: "A friend is someone who . . . " Ask each student to finish the sentence on a sheet of paper.

3. Next ask students to get in groups of five or six. Have one person write all six responses on one page. Have each group read their poem to the class.

4. Ask students for suggestions of ways to make new friends or improve relationships with the friends they already have. For example:

    Be friendly and smile.

    Be a good listener.

    Talk about the other person's interests.

    Do things together.

    Don't put people down.

5. Write each idea on the board and discuss. Ask students to try one of these ideas sometime during the week and report back to the group on how the idea worked.

Variations
1. Have students write a "wanted" classified advertisement for a friend. Include personal qualities, interests, and so forth. Discuss which is harder, to make new friends or to keep old friends.

2. Publish the group friendship poem in the school newspaper.

ACTIVITY 71

To Date or Not to Date?

Purpose   To encourage students to think critically about dating relationships

Materials   Paper and pencils

Procedure
1. Divide the class into small groups.

2. Ask the question "When is a teenager ready to date?" Have each small group brainstorm a list of responses.

3. Have the groups read their lists. Discuss what is common to all lists.

4. Ask the question "When do your parents think a teenager is ready to date?" Have each small group brainstorm a second list.

5. Again, have the groups share their lists. Discuss what is common to all lists.

6. Conduct a discussion comparing the students' beliefs with those of their parents. What responses are the same and where do the differences lie?

7. Ask the following discussion questions as time permits:

   What does it mean to date or "go with" someone?

   Why do people date? Is it the thing to do?

   Should parents be introduced to a new boyfriend or girlfriend?

   How do you go about asking for a date?

   Where do people go on dates?

   Should you go out on a blind date?

Love Is . . .

Purpose To help students think about the word *love* and what it means in a relationship

Materials Chalkboard
Paper and pencils

Procedure 1. Brainstorm on the board completions to the following sentence stems:

Love is . . .

Ways to express love include . . .

We show our love to . . .

2. Discuss the following ideas:

The difference between love and infatuation

How well you should know someone before going out or going with the person

How old you should be in order to date

What your parents say about dating

3. Ask students to write down any questions they have regarding boy-girl relationships and place them in a box to be discussed later.

Variation Have students ask their parents for their views about dating. Share during the next meeting.

Down in the Dumps

Purpose   To identify what makes people depressed and ways they can feel better

Materials   None

Procedure

1. Ask the group to identify some of the feelings or behaviors people have when they are depressed. Point out that it is normal for teenagers to experience low moods that relate to the turmoil of their age.

2. Discuss the following questions:

   What makes you feel down?

   Do your friends understand when you are in a bad mood?

   What effect does your mood have on those around you?

   What helps you get back in a good mood?

   When you are in a bad mood, how do you act?

3. Brainstorm a list of ways of dealing with depression. The list could include the following:

   Do something active with friends or family.

   Think about something you did for fun and do it again.

   Talk about it—share your feelings with someone who will just listen.

   Talk to a counselor.

   Sit down and try to figure out the cause of your feelings.

   Take a walk or get some other exercise.

   Draw, write a poem, sing.

   Hang on and try to stay in your routine.

4. Discuss with students which idea from the list might work best for them. Ask for a volunteer to try one of the suggestions and share at the next meeting how it went.

Variations

1. Discuss a movie in which the director takes you through several different mood changes. Is this type of drama necessary in making a quality film? Is life the same way?

2. List TV shows or videos that can improve your mood.

3. Read *The Fall of Freddie the Leaf*, by Leo Buscaglia (Holt, Rinehart and Winston, 1982). This short children's story concerns ways of dealing with death and loss.

Growing Up and Growing Old

Purpose To encourage students to think about growing up and the pros and cons of growing older

Materials Chalkboard

Procedure 1. Tell students that there are many benefits to being older. Ask them, "If you could be any age, what age would you like to be?"

2. Ask students to think of a few examples of an age when they will have an opportunity they currently do not have—for example, they can drive a car at 16, vote at 18, retire at age 65.

3. On the chalkboard, draw the following table:

	Pros	Cons
20–35		
36–50		
51–65		
66+		

4. Divide the group into four smaller groups. Have each one take a different age group and come up with at least five pros and five cons for it.

5. Have each group report their ideas and write them on the board. Discuss each category, emphasizing what students have to look forward to.

Variation Have students ask their parents to reflect on each category. Have them interview a grandparent or another elderly person and see how that person responds.

Sneak Attack

Purpose To encourage students to reflect on their responsibilities at home and help them understand what it means to be part of a family team

Materials None

Procedure 1. Go around the circle and ask students what type of chores and/or responsibilities they have at home. Ask what contributions they make to the family on a regular basis and what chores or responsibilities any of their brothers or sisters have at home.

2. Go around the circle again and ask students what type of responsibilities their parents make to keep the family unit working.

3. Have students think of one chore that another person in their family does on a regular basis. Ask the students to go home and make a "sneak attack" and do that chore without being asked and without anyone knowing.

4. Have students report back to the group the outcome of this "sneak attack."

Variations 1. Have students write a thank-you note to a parent and/or sibling for something this person routinely does.

2. Have students think of ways they can help out their families by taking on an additional responsibility for several weeks. Encourage them to watch to see how this might change family relationships.

ACTIVITY 76

Cultures in Your School

Purpose   To encourage awareness of different cultures in the school

Materials   Chalkboard

Procedure   1. Explain to students that we are all from different backgrounds. We are different in terms of race, religion, country of origin, or ethnic background. These differences are our cultural background.

2. Ask students to try to identify all the cultural groups within their school. List these on the chalkboard.

3. Go around the circle and ask students to identify their own cultural background. Ask them if most of their friends are from a similar background or from a different background.

4. Explain that we are all "culture-bound." That is, we believe in those practices that are acceptable and standard for the cultural group we identify with most closely. We generally choose to be with those who are most like us.

5. Encourage students to discuss why most of our close friends are from a similar culture. As time permits, ask the following discussion questions:

What is an example of how your culture is different from others (for example, values, language, dress, attitudes)?

What are some opportunities and problems that happen when you bring different cultural groups together?

Is it difficult for some people to accept others who are different from themselves? Why?

What are some things we can do to help others be more understanding and accepting of individual differences?

Pretend you are arriving in the United States for the first time. List as many traditions or customs as you can that might seem odd (for example, the Easter Bunny, fortunes in cookies, shopping malls).

Variation   Read *The Three Astronauts,* by U. Eco and E. Carmi (Harcourt Brace Jovanovich, 1989). This story concerns three astronauts of different nationalities who take off in separate rockets and meet on Mars. Discuss what the astronauts have in common and how they learn to live together.

We Are All Different

Purpose To help students understand individual differences and explore how they feel about race, gender, ethnic background, age, disability, and religion

Materials Chalkboard
Magazines
Scissors
Glue
Poster board
Markers

Procedure 1. On the chalkboard, write the following words: *race, gender, ethnic background, age, disability,* and *religion.* Discuss the meaning of each term and ask students to give examples of different groups under each. Discuss how people seem to react to these differences in others. Explain that it is common for people to feel awkward or uncomfortable about differences but that these feelings can be overcome with understanding.

2. Have students get into groups of three to five. Pass out magazines, scissors, glue, and a poster board to each group. Ask each group to cut out pictures of people who are different in the ways discussed. Have them write "We Are All Different" at the top of the poster board, then paste their pictures on the board as a collage.

3. Have groups share their collages. Post the collages around the room or in the hallways.

Variations 1. Ask students to interview a person from a racial or ethnic group different from their own. Ask them to try to identify at least three differences between their cultures or traditions.

2. Have students interview a person with a physical disability. Encourage students to find out how the disability affects the person's life and how the person copes with the challenge.

Countries of Origin

Purpose   To encourage students to try to determine the ethnic backgrounds of their families

Materials   World map
Push-pins
Chalkboard

Procedure   1. Explain to students that unless they are Native Americans, their family originated in a country or place other than here and that the people in the United States are a combination of many different cultural and ethnic backgrounds. Point out that in a family the mother's side of the family often has a country of origin different from the father's side of the family.

2. Tell students about your own ethnic background and the countries in which your ancestors originated. Locate these countries on the map.

3. Explain that we may be different on the outside but are the same on the inside. We are all a part of the human family. We are all connected, even to people we don't know. We may have cousins or other relatives who still live in other countries.

4. Give students two push-pins apiece. Ask them to go to the chalkboard and print their last names and then go to the world map and place the pins on the countries or places where their family members originated. Ask if they have ever visited the country. See if other students have any knowledge or ideas about the country. (If students are not sure about their backgrounds, they can ask a parent or family member and provide their information at a later session.)

Variations   1. If there are foreign students in the group or in your school, encourage group members to interview them about their countries (language, food, houses, religion, and so forth).

2. Invite guest speakers from other countries to address the group.

3. View a film about a country where members of your group have ancestors.

4. Have students bring special foods from their countries of origin.

Corner to Corner

Purpose To help students become more aware of their beliefs and accept the fact that different people hold different beliefs

Materials A sign reading "Agree" and a sign reading "Disagree," placed in opposite corners of the room

Procedure
1. Make a statement such as the following: "A woman should be President of the United States." Give the students a moment to think about the statement and to consider to what degree they believe it to be true. Ask them to go, on your signal, to the corner that has the sign coinciding with their belief.

2. Allow time for the students in each corner to discuss their reasons for choosing that particular answer. Call on each group to give the reason they chose that response.

3. Repeat the exercise with the following statements as time permits:

   Everyone should be required to graduate from high school in order to get a driver's license.

   Girls are smarter than boys.

   Students should have the right to choose their own dress code at home or at school.

   Giving grades encourages cheating.

   Women should be able to fly in military combat.

   The drinking age should be lowered to 16 years, and the driving age should be raised to 19 years.

4. Point out to students that there are no right or wrong corners to stand in. The world is made up of different people with different views.

Variation Ask students to pretend they are their parents and do the same exercise. How are their parents' views similar or different from theirs?

Tolerance

Purpose   To show that we all have different levels of tolerance for different things

Materials   Chalkboard

Procedure

1. Write on the chalkboard the word *tolerance*. Ask students to state any words they associate with tolerance. Elicit that tolerance is accepting certain things or people that you may not agree with.

2. Go around the circle and ask students to give an example of something they cannot tolerate and a time they exercised extreme tolerance.

3. Discuss the following questions:

   Do you think you are more tolerant or less tolerant than you were a year ago?

   Are you more tolerant or less tolerant than your family members?

4. Ask students to show thumbs-up if they agree and thumbs-down if they disagree with the following statements:

   I like shoulder-length hair on boys.

   I think it's OK for women to wear pants to work.

   I think it's OK for boys to wear earrings in both ears.

   I would vote for a woman President.

   I think it's OK for men to cry.

   I would share my lunch with someone I don't know.

   I think it's OK for a woman to be a truck driver.

   I think people should be drafted into the military.

   I would marry someone of a different race or religion.

   I think men are worse drivers than women.

5. Finally, ask students what can happen when people do not tolerate one another. Ask for examples they see around the school.

Reducing Prejudice

Purpose   To help students become more understanding of individual differences

Materials   A sign reading "Like Me" and a sign reading "Not Like Me," placed in opposite corners of the room

Procedure   1. Explain that we all have different backgrounds, interests, and beliefs. Point out that people will sometimes react to these differences with prejudice. When we prejudge a person because of age, gender, disability, appearance, social class, and so on, that is prejudice.

2. Ask students to volunteer times when they felt that someone prejudged them. Discuss.

3. Next explain that you will call out a number of characteristics or identities that students may or may not relate to. Students should go toward the "Like Me" sign if they relate to the identity. If they do not relate to the identity, they should go toward the "Not Like Me" sign. They can also stand anywhere in between the two signs to show the degree to which the characteristic is like or unlike them.

4. Read the following list, adding other identities to it as appropriate:

   Musical

   Recycler

   Shopper

   Studious

   Athletic

   Traveler

   Conservative

   Social

5. Have students return to their seats and process some of the following questions:

   What are the identities you have that you relate to most strongly?

   What are some of the ethnic and cultural backgrounds represented in the group?

   How did you feel when you were alone or with one other person standing by a sign?

   How did it feel to be in a group where you were in the majority? In the minority?

Variation   Have students line up according to physical characteristics. For example:

Tallest to shortest

Biggest feet to smallest feet

Darkest hair to lightest hair

Lightest skin to darkest skin

Longest hair to shortest hair

Discuss how it feels to be placed in line according to physical traits.

Sex-Role Stereotypes

Purpose To encourage students' learning about stereotypes and how such stereotypes relate to gender expectations

Materials Chalkboard

Procedure 1. Ask students if they think boys or girls have it easier in the world. Encourage examples and diverse opinions.

2. On the chalkboard, write: "Boys are . . . " and "Girls are . . . " Have students brainstorm a list of so-called male traits and female traits under each heading.

3. Discuss what types of generalizations can be made about each list.

4. Define *stereotype* as a fixed notion or idea about a person or group—an oversimplified generalization of a person or group. Give the following example: "Girls are emotional and like to take care of children" and "Boys are strong, rational thinkers and in control." Ask students if they think this stereotype has anything to do with why a female has never been President of the United States.

5. Discuss the negative effects of stereotyping. Include these ideas:

    It is the basis for prejudice.

    It is limiting.

    It is not true for all individuals.

    It is the basis for many conflicts.

6. Discuss ways students can overcome stereotyping. Ask the girls what the hardest thing is about being a boy; ask the boys what the hardest thing is about being a girl.

Variation Discuss different stereotypes of various ethnic and racial groups. List a particular group and brainstorm some of the generalizations people make about the group. Discuss if these generalizations are true and how you can change existing images of people or groups.

Words for Discussion

FRIEND

Personalize   What are the most important qualities you want in a friend?

How do you choose a friend? How do you lose a friend?

Share a situation in which you were let down by a friend.

Have you ever let a friend down? Why?

Define   Friend = An acquaintance whom one knows well and cherishes; one attached to another by affection or esteem.

Challenge   Send a note to a good friend to affirm the friendship.

If you had to decide whether to go to a school dance with your best friend or with a date, which would you choose? Why?

LYING

Personalize   When did you get in trouble for lying? What would have happened if you had told the truth?

Give an example of a time someone lied to you. How did this make you feel? How did it change your relationship?

How long does it take for trust to be reestablished after a lie?

Define   Lying = The habit of telling misinformation; untruthfulness, deceit, deception, falsehood.

Challenge   Think of a person to whom you have lied or a situation in which you have lied and think of a different way to handle it. Is it ever OK to lie? Give examples.

CLIQUE

Personalize   List all the cliques in the school.

Why do some students closely identify with certain groups and others want no group identity?

What are the similarities and differences between a gang and a clique (clothes, neighborhoods, interests)?

Define   Clique = An exclusive or clannish group of people.

Challenge   Imagine for a day that you hung around with a totally different clique—one that you would usually never be with. Try it!

Sit at a totally different table at lunch or invite someone who is from a different group to eat at your table.

PEER PRESSURE

Personalize   Give an example of a time peer pressure resulted in something positive and also in something negative.

Does peer pressure come from your peers, or does it come from you and your need to be a part of the group?

When you are feeling peer pressure, how well does "Just say no" work?

Define   Peer pressure = Forceful persuasion exerted by one's peers.

Challenge   Think of a situation in which you could pressure a friend to do something positive that the person normally wouldn't do.

Give examples of ways to resist peer pressure.

LOVE

Personalize   Love is . . .

How do you know if you are in love?

How do you show your love to family or friends?

Is love more than a feeling? What responsibilities are involved in a relationship based on love?

Define   Love = A strong affection; deep devotion; great interest or fondness; attachment.

Challenge   Write a note to your parents to tell them you love them.

List five people you love. Beside each, write a responsibility you have as part of the loving relationship.

LOSS

Personalize   Share a loss you have experienced (friendship, death of a loved one, death of a pet, a move).

How did you feel about the loss (anger, denial, depression, unfairness)?

Define   Loss = The removal of something valued by a person—for example, by accident or death.

172

Challenge Think of a friend who has lost something important. Think about how that person is feeling. Do or say something to try to help the person handle the loss.

DEPRESSION

Personalize Think of a time you felt depressed. What do you think caused your depression?

Do you think depression is something you can't help or behaviors and feelings you choose?

When your friends or family members seem depressed or upset, what have you tried to do or say to help the situation?

Define Depression = Low spirits or vitality; feelings of low energy, dejection, and despair.

Challenge Make a list of 10 things you could do if you or someone you know is feeling depressed.

TELEVISION

Personalize How many hours a day do you spend in front of the TV (includes cable, Nintendo, videos)?

What are some of the positives and negatives about TV viewing?

What would happen to your family if there was no TV?

Define Television = An optical electric system for continuous transmission of visual images and sound.

Challenge Watch TV for one night and write down the number of acts of violence and the number of sexual encounters over a 3-hour period. What lessons do you learn from TV?

Did you know that children average 6 hours each day of TV? Go for one week without watching TV and see what effects this has on your life.

ADVERTISEMENT

Personalize Give an example of one of your favorite TV advertisements—an ad that really sticks in your mind.

What messages or images do advertisements relate to you?

When Nike says, "Just do it," do you? Is this a negative advertisement? Is it effective?

Do you agree or disagree that beer advertisements should be taken off TV?

173

Define   Advertisement = A message to make known the qualities of a product, generally in order to sell.

Challenge   Watch TV for a 2-hour period one night and write down each product that is advertised. Share your list. How does your list relate to what you or your parents buy?

MONEY

Personalize   How do you get your money (job, allowance, ask for it)?

If you won 25,000 dollars in the lottery, what would you do with the money?

When can having too much money be a problem? How do you feel about people with more money than you?

What is most important: money, happiness, or friendship?

Define   Money = Whatever serves as the common medium of exchange.

Challenge   Is there something expensive that you've been wanting to buy? What are some ways for you to make the money?

Keep track of the money you spend in a week; develop a budget for a month.

UNIT SIX

Your Community

Unless we change our direction, we are likely to end up where we are headed.

Old Chinese Proverb

Overview

Every student is a member of the school community as well as the larger community. One goal of education is for young people to learn about their communities and to become contributing members of society. Many schools across the country are requiring community service projects as part of the overall educational program.

The activities in this unit help students acquire specific knowledge of community needs and resources. Recreational, health care, commercial, employment, and counseling opportunities are available in most areas. However, students cannot access services and resources within the community if they do not understand what exists.

Another aspect of community membership is making contributions that help others and increase the quality of life for community members. Many personal needs can also be met through community service. Thus, activities are designed to help students increase their feelings of responsibility, self-worth, and independence through personal contributions.

Activities

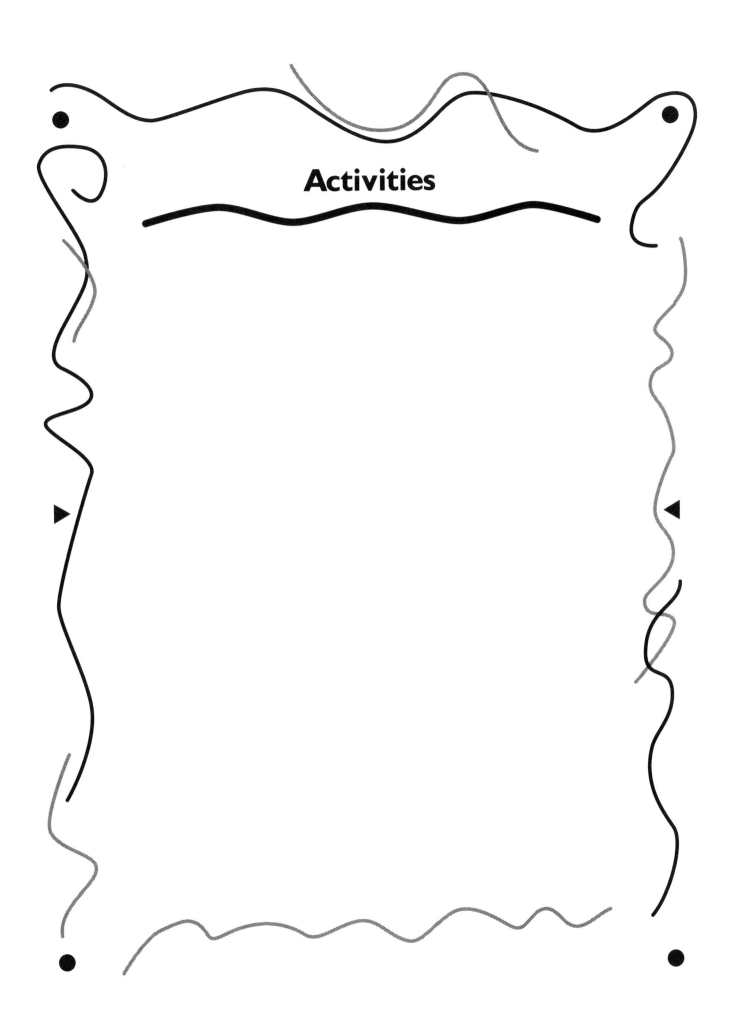

Community Research

Purpose To encourage students to research the various social service programs and organizations serving the community

Materials Chalkboard
Telephone books (as needed)
Telephone
Paper and pencils

Procedure
1. Write the following four categories on the board: medical, recreational, counseling, and crisis. Ask students to name any programs or agencies they know of under each category. Question students as to what specific information they know and do not know about each agency.

2. Have students get into groups of three and choose a program or agency they would like to find out more about. Encourage students to look the program or agency up in the telephone book and develop 5 to 10 questions that they will use to conduct a telephone survey. For example:

County Blood Bank

What days and hours is the blood bank open?

How old do you have to be before you can donate?

Is the blood bank in need of any particular blood types at this time? If so, which ones?

Where is the blood bank located?

Does the blood bank offer any jobs for teens? If so, what?

Where does the blood go after it is collected?

Nursing Home

What is the name of the nursing home?

Where is it located?

How old do you have to be to live there?

How much is it per month to live there?

Does the nursing home offer jobs for teens? If so, what?

What special services are offered to residents?

How can the nursing home use volunteers?

Emergency Shelter

What is the name of the shelter?

Where is it located?

Whom does it serve?

How many beds does it have?

Does the shelter have any rules? If so, name two.

Does the shelter offer jobs for teens? If so, what?

What types of donations or volunteers are needed?

Boys and Girls Club

Where is the club located?

What age kids can join?

What type of activities are available?

What does it cost?

How does someone sign up?

3. Have students telephone the agency they chose and ask their survey questions.

4. During the next group time, have students report their findings.

Variations
1. Visit some of the places you discussed.

2. Invite guest speakers from the agencies you researched.

3. Share this information with others in the school.

4. Have a grade-level assembly informing other students of the information gained.

Public Officials in Your Community

Purpose   To encourage awareness of elected and appointed officials and their responsibilities to the community

Materials   Chalkboard
Telephone books (as needed)
Butcher paper
Markers

Procedure   1. Have students brainstorm the offices of local public officials—for example, mayor, police chief, fire chief, superintendent of schools, state representative, school board member, county board member, city clerk, and city council member. Write these on the chalkboard.

2. Have each student use the telephone book to find out how to call one of these people, then have the student call to find out what responsibilities the person has. Information to collect includes the name of each official, his or her job title, a short job description, and whether the person is elected or appointed.

3. During the next class, have students write their information on the butcher paper. Post the list in the room.

4. During the school year, whenever a local official is mentioned in the newspaper, have students cut the article out and attach it to the butcher paper under that person's name. (If it is an election year, you will probably have to revise the list as new people are elected or appointed.)

Variations   1. Take a field trip to visit a public official at work.

2. Invite public officials to the class as guest speakers.

3. Write letters to public officials providing praise and suggestions.

4. Repeat this activity with leaders from the business community.

Using the Yellow Pages

Purpose   To give students the opportunity to become familiar with the yellow pages of the telephone book

Materials   Telephone books (as needed)
Yellow Pages Trivia (Handout 21)

Procedure   1. Discuss with students how they have used the yellow pages in the telephone book. Share with them situations in which you have personally relied on the yellow pages for guidance.

2. Give each group of four students a telephone book to examine. Compare the yellow pages and the white pages. How are they the same and how are they different?

3. After students have some understanding of the yellow pages, pass out the Yellow Pages Trivia worksheet (Handout 21). You may need to adapt this worksheet to fit your situation. Have students answer the questions on this sheet in small groups.

4. When students are finished, discuss the results in the larger group.

Variation   Develop an interdisciplinary unit using the yellow pages:

Use words found in the yellow pages as spelling or vocabulary words.

Develop math problems by using numbers found in the yellow pages.

For science, focus on the different types of doctors available.

For social studies, use the maps included.

For art, draw an advertisement for one of the merchants listed.

For language arts/music, write and sing a jingle for a merchant or agency.

For home economics, try recipes from local ethnic restaurants listed.

YELLOW PAGES TRIVIA

1. List different public transportation services our city or town offers.

2. Pretend you just moved here and you get a serious toothache. Which dentist do you decide on and why?

3. I need to make a copy of my science report. Give me three different places where I could go to make copies.

4. Aunt Julie agrees to buy you a new bike as long as you go for the best quality at the best price. Where would you call?

5. Where would you call if you needed a swimming instructor?

6. Where are the locations for recycling in town?

7. Are there more lawyers or insurance salespeople in town?

8. Are there more ice cream stores or weight-loss centers?

9. Use the map and analyze why McDonalds has selected the particular locations it has.

10. State one thing you like and dislike about using the yellow pages.

Social Agencies to Know

Purpose   To introduce and discuss the services of various social agencies found in your community

Materials   Chalkboard
Telephone books (as needed)
Social Agencies to Know (Handout 22)

Procedure   1. Discuss with students the everyday problems that can occur in one's life. List these problems on the chalkboard.

2. Pass out telephone books (or copies of the social services section contained in the yellow pages). Discuss the various agencies that can be of help. You may need to emphasize particular agencies about which students have no previous knowledge.

3. After students have an understanding of these organizations, break them into groups of three. Provide each group with one Social Agencies to Know worksheet (Handout 22) and see how well they do in answering the questions. (You may need to adapt the worksheet to suit your own community.)

4. In the larger group, discuss the responses the teams gave on their worksheets.

Variations 1. Adopt one of these agencies for your group and do a volunteer project during the school year.

2. Develop a "Youth Yellow Pages" and publish it in the school newsletter or newspaper.

3. Read and discuss the story *Cracker Jackson*, by Betsy Byars (G. K. Hall, 1987). In this story, Cracker Jackson tries to help a friend with a tough problem of physical abuse.

SOCIAL AGENCIES TO KNOW

1. What telephone number would you call in a medical crisis?

2. What is the name and telephone number of the agency responsible for child abuse reports?

3. Where is the county mental health office located?

4. Name two places you can donate clothing for needy families.

5. What is the name and location of the food bank?

6. List the name and addresses of three emergency shelters in the community.

7. If an elderly person needed meals brought into his or her home, what agency could help them?

8. What is the telephone number for Al-Anon? When and where do they meet?

9. What is the name and telephone number of a youth employment program?

10. Who is your state representative? Where is his or her office, and what is the telephone number?

11. State the purpose of the American Red Cross.

12. Suppose that in science class you're doing a report on leukemia. What organization can you call to get information?

Recreational Fun

Purpose To encourage students to investigate recreational facilities in the community

Materials Paper and pencils
Chalkboard

Procedure 1. Ask students what they do for fun.

2. Divide the group into teams of three or four. Give each team a piece of paper and have them assign a recorder. The recorder is to make two lists of all the places or activities that are fun and safe for teens and/or their families to go. One list is headed "Free" and the other list is headed "Cost." See which team can come up with the most ideas.

3. Have recorders for each team share with the larger group the outcomes of the brainstorming session. List on the chalkboard all the places students could think of going. You may need to suggest places the students did not come up with, such as the library, YMCA, museums, or parks.

4. Discuss the free versus cost activities. What is students' favorite place to go? Why?

5. Ask students to go to a new free activity and report back to the class how they liked it.

Variations 1. Tell the class there is a storm coming and only three recreational facilities will remain. Have students debate which three they most want to remain.

2. Rank order the activities listed. Go and visit one of the top three spots.

3. Provide coupons from one of the locations as a student incentive.

Discovering New Careers

Purpose   To make students aware of different possible careers

Materials   Career Match Job Descriptions (Handout 23)
Slips of paper, previously prepared with different career titles

Procedure   1. Write the following career titles on separate slips of paper, then fold them and place them in a hat. Have each student draw one slip out of the hat.

Podiatrist

Optometrist

Chiropractor

Arbitrator

Mortician

Horticulturist

Aviator

Superintendent of schools

Mycologist

Pathologist

Illustrator

Admiral

2. Give each student a copy of the Career Match Job Descriptions form (Handout 23). Have students circulate around the room asking other students questions like "Are you a foot doctor?" "Do you fly an airplane?" If the student says no, then nothing happens. Students continue to circulate until careers are found for each job description. When a student finds a career, he or she writes it on the line provided next to the description. (Students who do not know what their career title means will need time to look it up in a dictionary.) Ask students to sit down as they complete the activity so you will know when everyone is finished.

3. After all students are seated, discuss the following questions with the class:

What new careers have you discovered?

Would you like to have one of these as your job some day?

What kind of schooling do you think each job requires?

What kind of income do you think these people make?

Variations 1. Invite people in the various careers to be guest speakers.

2. Encourage students to interview people who have these careers.

3. Have parents come to the group to discuss their careers.

CAREER MATCH JOB DESCRIPTIONS

Takes care of people's feet _____

Takes care of people's eyes _____

Treats back and neck injuries _____

Settles disputes or conflicts _____

Prepares the dead and manages funerals _____

Works with plants _____

Flies airplanes _____

Directs the school district _____

Works with fungi _____

Studies the causes and nature of death _____

Makes drawings and designs _____

Commands ships in the navy _____

ACTIVITY 89

What's My Career?

Purpose To have students become aware of a variety of careers

Materials Chalkboard
Index cards
Tape

Procedure 1. For 3 minutes, have students brainstorm a list of careers. Write these on the chalkboard. Have a student write each career on a separate index card. Be sure to have at least one card per student. Some examples include attorney, doctor, dentist, teacher, mail carrier, salesperson, ecologist, engineer, manager, maintenance person, grocer, waiter, undertaker, construction worker, truck driver, taxi driver, nurse, electrician, plumber, artist, carpenter, welder, lawn care specialist, and receptionist.

2. Erase the board. Tape a card to each student's back without letting the student see it. Have students mingle, asking one another about the occupations taped to their own backs. Questions may vary, but students may give only yes-and-no answers. When students have determined who they are, tell them to put the name tags on their fronts and go back to their seats.

Variations 1. Have one student at a time get a card taped to his or her back. Have that student play "20 Questions" to try to find out what the career is. Again, only yes-and-no responses are allowed.

2. Invite adults whom the students do not know. Have the students play the same game, trying to determine what the adult really does for a living. (This is like the old TV game show "What's My Line.")

Adopt a Group

Purpose To teach social responsibility through volunteer service

Materials Vary with the project chosen

Procedure NOTE: Whatever project you decide to undertake, have fun doing it. There is a great possibility this project will create pride and enhance self-worth.

1. Create an awareness of community needs by brainstorming with students places that could benefit from students' commitment and involvement. Possibilities include nursing homes, elementary schools, facilities for people with disabilities, charities, food banks, and parks.

2. Discuss with students which of these community needs they would like to try to meet during the semester or school year. Take into consideration the difficulties of transportation. If you are within walking distance of the facility, it will be easier to get to the site.

3. After your group has agreed upon a volunteer project to adopt, call the organization to see if your students can be of help. If so, have someone from that program come to your class and tell how community needs are addressed as well as how the students can be of help.

Example Projects

Parks: You may first write the park district to inform them of your interest and possible plans. Ideas include picking up trash, sweeping, planting a tree, assisting park officials with flowers, and so on.

Elementary schools: Contact a specific teacher to discuss how your students can act as tutors. This would include working on math facts, reading books, helping in story writing, acting as "pen pals" by writing back and forth, aiding in an art project, or leading games on the playground.

Nursing homes: Meet the public relations person and introduce your ideas. A wide range of projects can be part of this adoption. Some are interviewing residents and writing their life stories, making holiday decorations with or for residents, taking a "walk and talk," reading aloud, performing skits and songs, making crafts together, or making a video together. These experiences will be cherished by many.

Our School Community

Purpose To help students develop ownership of and responsibility toward their school by offering their special skills or interests to others

Materials Vary with the project chosen

Procedure
1. Ask students how they would like to participate in helping others at their school. Students may be unaware of certain duties and tasks that are needed in order for the school to function.

2. Each building will have its own needs. The students should look around and assess what those needs are. Have them come up with a project and clear it with the principal. If you can't think of any ideas, ask the principal. He or she may have something special for you to do.

Example Projects

School secretaries often spend countless hours preparing the school newsletter. See if students could help fold, staple, and put on mailing labels.

Unclaimed clothing in the lost and found might need to be washed and bagged and donated to the area clothing room or to a community help organization.

Library shelves or a display case might need dusting. Offer to dust once a month in the library.

When is the last time the desks were cleaned? Ask the custodial staff for the necessary cleaning supplies.

Adopt a hallway. Keep it clean and decorated for the month.

Seasonal Events

Purpose   To develop a sense of community through volunteer projects with seasonal themes

Materials   Vary with the project chosen

Procedure
1. Ask students to think of the next three seasonal events that are approaching. Have them think of activities and traditions that are part of these events.
2. Next ask students to think of the special needs the school and community have during these seasonal times. Ask them if they are willing to take on an event as part of a seasonal/holiday volunteer service project. Be creative in meeting the needs of your building and community. For example:

Fall

Rake leaves for a senior citizen who lives near school.

Collect and repair toys for needy children.

Provide tour guides for the fall open house.

Collect canned goods for needy families at Thanksgiving.

Create a spook house for smaller children to tour.

Write a book of Halloween poems for the local library.

Winter

Shovel the sidewalk at school.

A few minutes before school is dismissed, scrape the ice off staff cars.

Make valentines to decorate the library.

Design a showcase for Black History Month (February).

Draw posters supporting a special event, dance, concert, or game.

Decorate a hallway bulletin board in honor of Women in History Month (March).

Write an article for the local newspaper about Dr. Martin Luther King.

Spring

Plant flowers in front of the school.

Pull weeds around the school.

Offer a spring cleaning in the locker rooms.

Help return lost and found items.

Dust out the trophy case.

Make a video on why moms are special and invite mothers in for viewing. Have doughnuts with fathers another day.

Organize an all-school assembly to thank staff for their contributions.

Fund-Raisers

Purpose   To have students raise money for a worthwhile cause

Materials   Vary with the project chosen

Procedure   NOTE: None of the ideas suggested in this activity is designed to sell things or make a large amount of money. The idea is mainly for students to make a financial contribution to a community group that helps needy people. Donating the money to a local charity not only enhances the school climate but also improves school-community relationships.

1. Ask your group if they would like to have a small fund-raising event and donate the proceeds to one of the local service projects or agencies that they have learned about.

2. If a large majority of the students are enthusiastic, ask them first to set a goal for the amount they would like to donate.

3. Next ask students what organization, agency, or project they wish to donate the money to. Animal shelters, libraries, homeless shelters, parks, and other charities or nonprofit organizations will truly appreciate your donations.

4. Students can now use their planning skills to decide how to raise the money, the steps and timeline, and what materials they will need. Try to involve every student in the group with a task or responsibility. Fund-raising ideas include recycling cans, conducting a penny drive, washing cars, and having students hire themselves out for chores. Having a school dance can be a quick, if labor-intensive, way to bring in money.

Variation   Expand the penny-drive project to the whole school. Classrooms might compete to see which group can collect the most pennies.

Community Letter Writing

Purpose To have students share with others their thoughts and feelings of appreciation through letters

Materials Stationery and pens
Envelopes
Stamps

Procedure 1. Ask students how they feel when they get a personal letter mailed to them and what they like to read about in a letter.

2. Discuss with students the feeling of appreciation, how nice it is to show appreciation to others in a letter, and how to compose a friendly letter.

3. Ask students to think of someone in the community who would like to receive a letter of appreciation. If students are having difficulty determining whom to write, give them some ideas:

Think of a specific incident in which you were helped by someone (the roller skating manager, the librarian).

Think of someone with whom you are in agreement about a particular issue. Write that person (mayor, state representative) and give your support. (It is also good to write a letter about an issue you disagree on, stating why.)

Think of a person who has taken a special interest in you (your neighbors, former teacher). Write and tell that person how much you appreciate his or her kind words and support.

Think of a person who always smiles at you and makes you feel good no matter what (piano teacher, coach).

Think of people who do good things for others in your community (fire fighters, parks department staff).

4. Writing letters and having regular correspondence with others is an important life skill. Continue to encourage students by giving them time to write others.

Variation Encourage students to write a letter at least once a month. Some other people who would appreciate receiving letters include their oldest relative, a relative who lives far away, a person in prison, someone their age living in a foreign country, someone in a hospital, and so on.

References and Bibliography

Beane, J., & Lipka, R. (1987). *When the kids come first: Enhancing self-esteem.* Columbus, OH: National Middle School Association.

Canfield, J., & Wells, H. (1976). *100 ways to enhance self-concept in the classroom.* Englewood Cliffs, NJ: Prentice-Hall.

Carnegie Council on Adolescent Development. (1989). *Turning points: Preparing American youth for the 21st century.* Washington, DC: Carnegie Corporation.

Crum, T. (1987). *The magic of conflict.* New York: Touchstone/Simon & Schuster.

Drew, N. (1987). *Learning the skills of peacemaking.* Rolling Hills Estates, CA: Jalmar.

Fisher, R., & Ury, W. (1981). *Getting to yes: Negotiating agreement without giving in.* New York: Penguin.

Fluegelman, A. (Ed.). (1976). *The new games book.* Garden City, NY: Dolphin/Doubleday.

Frey, D., & Carlock C. (1984). *Enhancing self-esteem.* Muncie, IN: Accelerated Development.

Glasser, W. (1986). *Control theory in the classroom.* New York: Harper and Row.

Glasser, W. (1990). *The quality school.* New York: Harper & Row.

Goldstein, A., Reagles, K., & Amann, L. (1990). *Refusal skills: Preventing drug use in adolescents.* Champaign, IL: Research Press.

Goldstein, A., Sprafkin, R., Gershaw, N., & Klein, P. (1980). *Skillstreaming the adolescent: A structured learning approach to teaching prosocial skills.* Champaign, IL: Research Press.

James, M. (1986). *Adviser-advisee programs: Why, what and how.* Columbus, OH: National Middle School Association.

Johnson, D., & Johnson, F. (1975). *Joining together.* Englewood Cliffs, NJ: Prentice Hall.

Kreidler, W. (1984). *Creative conflict resolution.* Glenview, IL: Scott, Foresman.

Kreidler, W. (1990). *Teaching concepts of peace and conflict.* Cambridge, MA: Educators for Social Responsibility.

Morganett, R. (1990). *Skills for living: Group counseling activities for young adolescents.* Champaign, IL: Research Press.

National Association of Secondary School Principals. (1985). *An agenda for excellence at the middle school level.* Reston, VA: Author.

National Middle School Association. (1982). *This we believe.* Columbus, OH: Author.

Schrader, J. (1990). *Boundary breakers.* Reston, VA: National Association of Secondary School Principals.

Schrumpf, F., Crawford, D., & Usadel, C. (1991). *Peer mediation: Conflict resolution in schools* (Program Guide and Student Manual). Champaign, IL: Research Press.

Schrumpf, F. (1991). *Home room advisory teacher resource manual.* Urbana, IL: Urbana School District 116.

Stock, G. (1988). *The kid's book of questions.* New York: Working Publishing.

Van Hoose, J. (1991). The ultimate goal: A/A across the day. *Midpoints, 2*(1), 1–7.

About the Authors

Fred Schrumpf holds master's degrees in both social work and education from the University of Illinois at Urbana-Champaign. He has practiced school social work for the past 20 years. He has also taught at the University of Illinois, Eastern Washington University, and Idaho State University. He is currently a trainer-consultant delivering workshops on conflict resolution, peer mediation, and the teaching of life skills. In 1990 he was named Social Worker of the Year by the Illini chapter of the National Association of Social Workers. He is the coauthor of *Peer Mediation: Conflict Resolution in Schools* (Research Press, 1991).

Sharon Freiburg holds a master's degree in educational administration from the University of Illinois at Urbana-Champaign and a bachelor's of science degree in elementary education and special education from Quincy College, Quincy, Illinois. She has taught both regular and special education classes at various grade levels and has conducted workshops and inservices for school districts throughout Illinois on topics such as classroom management, cooperative learning, working with parents, and advisor-advisee programs. Currently, she is Dean of Students at Urbana High School in Urbana, Illinois.

David Skadden holds a bachelor's degree in education and master's degrees in both sports psychology and social work from the University of Illinois at Urbana-Champaign. He has taught and coached at the kindergarten through college levels. Presently, he is the school social worker at Central High School in Champaign, Illinois.